Foreign-Exchange Management in U.S. Multinationals

Foreign-Exchange Management in U.S. Multinationals

Rita M. Rodriguez
University of Illinois
at Chicago Circle

LexingtonBooks
D.C. Heath and Company
Lexington, Massachusetts
Toronto

182772

658.15
R 696f

Library of Congress Cataloging in Publication Data

Rodriguez, Rita M   1944-
   Foreign-exchange management in U.S. multinationals.

   Bibliography: p.
   Includes index.
   1. Foreign   exchange   administration.   2. Corporations,   American-
Finance. 3. International business enterprises—Finance. I. Title.
HG3851.R64   658.1'5   78-54708
ISBN 0-669-02330-2

Copyright © 1980 by D.C. Heath and Company.

All rights reserved. No part of this publication may be reproduced or
transmitted in any form or by any means, electronic or mechanical,
including photocopy, recording, or any information storage or retrieval
system, without permission in writing from the publisher.

Published simultaneously in Canada.

Printed in the United States of America.

International Standard Book Number: 0-669-02330-2

Library of Congress Catalog Card Number: 78-54708

TO HUSBAND

who will answer any further
questions on this book

Contents

List of Figures
and Tables

Preface

This book reports the findings of a research project that investigated the practices of U.S. multinational companies (MNCs) in the area of foreign-exchange management. The objectives of the book are twofold: to create a better understanding of the managerial process involved in the exchange-management decision and to assess the impact of these decisions on international financial markets.

The project was initiated in late 1973 at a time when the revised exchange parities of the Smithsonian Agreement of 1971 had failed. The system of generalized floating rates developed in March 1973 also appeared to be failing. Floating exchange rates so far had proven to be unstable exchange rates.

Attempts to explain the instability of the market quickly spotlighted the MNCs. Because they had the financial power to destabilize the market, MNCs began to be accused of being a major factor behind the markets' instability. MNCs complained they were not responsible for the state of affairs and, furthermore, they found it very difficult to operate in this uncertain environment. Attempts to sort out the role of MNCs in the exchange markets quickly revealed that no data were publicly available showing the positions of these companies in different currencies. In addition, the foreign-exchange management procedure followed by these companies was poorly understood. The goal of this project was to help fill this vacuum in information.

Although several years have elapsed since this investigation was initiated, not much has changed in the scenario that triggered it. Exchange markets are as unstable as ever. The European countries are again trying to maintain a system of fixed exchange rates among them reminiscent of the "snake" of 1973. Data on the exchange positions (specially defined) of U.S. MNCs has been published by the U.S. Treasury since 1977, but the decision process behind these figures is still poorly understood. The findings presented in this book, although based on data corresponding to an earlier period, should contribute to the understanding of the current situation.

This project involved protracted efforts on my part while I continued a virtually full-time course development and teaching schedule. First, I designed questionnaires and tested them as discussed in the book. These questionnaires were designed to help assemble the data needed. I also established a form for interviewing to elicit comments regarding the general goals of the international financial managers of the MNCs. The questionnaire was then administered by me to one or more managers of seventy U.S. multinationals throughout the United States over an eighteen-month period, with follow-up interviews three years later.

The quantitative exchange position data provided by most companies then had to be transferred to common data forms, validated and corrected, given the inevitable transmission errors, and formatted for various program processing. At one point, I determined there were over 64,000 data observations per company, which I had assembled.

Interpreting the output, discussing my tentative conclusions with managers, government officials, and academics resulted in further processing and analysis. Although I am aware of a variety of additional statistical analyses which could be conducted, I feel the limited number of firms in each currency and account make even small-sample, nonparametric tests rather useless. I prefer to rely on rough interpretation of the data as colored by the interview information, as discussed in the chapters.

Professor Raymond Vernon was not only instrumental in securing the initial outside funding for the project, but also encouraged me with his incisive questions and cheerful skepticism about management and academic pronouncements alike. My thanks to him for his patience and insight.

Special thanks are also given to the many financial officers who collaborated in this project and who gave so generously of their time.

Many operating personnel at the Harvard Computing Center assisted in many ways at odd hours over several years to move the project along. Dennis Robinson possessed unfailing good humor as he endured the seemingly endless revisions of programs and the invasion of his office space by my computer output. Bill Madison provided logistical support and coordination of operations which was invaluable, and made the computer facilities an almost limitless resource.

Several research assistants and secretaries worked serially and simultaneously to assemble and process the exchange and interview data. Among them Adam Blistein, Ann Lenton, Susan Esher, and Dev Purkayastha were particularly helpful. My thanks to them for their efforts. Other people provided no help or hindered the project, such as the programmer who could not find any computer, military or civilian, large enough to contain her program; and the academic administrator whose arrogance was exceeded only by his incompetence. It is a tribute to the others associated with the project that we all survived people such as these.

Initial funding for the project came from the Rockefeller Foundation. Although the results were published years later than they expected, I appreciate their support. Harvard Business School provided release time for a small fraction of the five calendar years on this project. I provided substantial additional funding to support this project in the manner I felt was required for an adequate completion of the research. Husband and daughter contributed the rest.

1 Introduction

The final collapse of the system of fixed exchange rates in 1973 ratified the existence of a new reality. The stability which the fixed exchange rate regime of the Bretton Woods Agreement had brought to the postwar period was over. For years, many economists had predicted that floating rates would both eliminate the need for exchange crises and be stable. Floating rates had arrived, but rate stability was yet to be seen. In fairness to the floating rate system, it must also be said that quadrupling of oil prices, world inflation, and other maladies of the 1970s also had arrived, still exchange rate instability appeared to be the new international (dis)order. For the financial manager of the multinational company, this environment demanded that one learning to cope with an exchange system which at times was capable of wild gyrations.

In a world of fixed exchange rates, the fact that different sovereign nations insist on having their own currencies represents a minor nuisance. The postwar period was a bit more complicated: fixed rates were not always constant. Most currencies changed their parities against the U.S. dollar during the 1945-1970 period. However, with a few exceptions, the parity changes had a kind of predictability to them—by and large they involved developing countries, and they represented exchange depreciations against the U.S. dollar. So, to the extent that U.S. managers worried about foreign-exchange risk, this meant protecting the value of their companies' foreign assets against depreciations in foreign currencies. By the end of the 1960s this state of affairs was coming to an end.

Table 1-1 shows the magnitudes of the changes in the spot rates of the currencies of major developed countries from December 1970 to September 1973. During this period all major currencies, except the U.S. dollar, managed to experience periods of strength. Even relatively weak currencies (the British pound, the Italian lira, and the Canadian dollar) often appreciated against the U.S. dollar during the period. And, even when these currencies depreciated against the U.S. dollar, they did so by a small amount relative to the overall depreciation of the U.S. dollar. The world of currencies in which financial managers operated in the 1970s had changed drastically from the earlier postwar period.

For government policymakers the international financial world also had changed. The days when government intervention—usually accompanied by appropriate changes in domestic policy—had shored up exchange crises appeared to be over. The recurrent nature of the exchange crises and their increasing intensity defied treatment by the conventional methods of the "good old days"

1

Table 1-1
Percentage Changes in Spot Rates of Major Currencies against the U.S. Dollar, December 1970 to September 1973

	French Franc	German Mark	Lira	Pound	Swiss Franc	Guilder	Belgian Franc	Yen	Canadian Dollar
December 1970-June 1971	–	+4.14	–	+1.09	+5.07	+1.00	–	–	-1.30
June 1971-December 1971	+5.28	+6.55	+4.74	+5.48	+4.44	+8·72	+10.05	+11.92	+2.07
December 1971-June 1972	+4.25	+3.42	+2.23	-4.24	+3.60	+2.49	+2.05	+4.35	+1.69
September 1972-March 1973	+9.40	+11.37	-0.11	+2.37	+14.84	+9.02	+9.28	+11.72	-1.59
March 1973-September 1973	+6.40	+14.73	+3.18	-2.59	+6.64	+13.89	+7.93	+3.80	-0.68

of fixed exchange rates. In fact, the adoption of the generalized system of floating rates in 1973 was nothing more than the governments' recognition of their
inability (and unwillingness) to defend exchange parities from the onslaughts
of the market.

The U.S. multinational companies (MNCs), which by now had been accused
of all kinds of wrongdoings, ranging from exploiting foreign countries to depos-
ing foreign governments, began to be suspected also of being behind the
recurring exchange crises. The large financial power that MNCs wield and the
manner in which they could exercise such power, it was argued, were a major
destabilizing factor in the international monetary system. Of course, business
retorted that their contribution to monetary upheaval had not been significant
and that whatever participation they had in the international capital flows
was not of a speculative nature. Rather, they argued, their actions were designed
solely to defend business interests in the face of fluctuations in monetary values.

By 1973 it was clear that the debate as to the role of the MNCs in exchange
crises, although rich in rhetoric, was short on empirical evidence. Data were
not even available publicly to analyze the problem.[1]

The dearth of empirical data on the role of MNCs in the exchange markets
prompted the staff of the Subcommittee on Multinational Corporations of the
U.S. Senate to begin a study of this area.[2] In this study the currency positions
in various accounts of 56 U.S. multinationals were compiled for January, February, and March in 1972 and 1973. Two consecutive devaluations of the U.S.
dollar had occurred during February and March 1973. It was expected that
a comparison of the companies' positions during the exchange crises with their
positions the earlier year—a period of calmer exchange markets—would provide
information as to whether these companies contributed to the dollar devaluations. To see whether these companies had transferred funds from dollars
into the currencies which appreciated against the dollar, the currency positions
were compiled separately for the so-called strong currencies (German mark,
yen, Swiss franc, and guilder). Other currencies were segregated into two groups:
"other Europeans" and "all others."

Since the actions by different companies often cancelled each other out,
the study could not attribute a significant role to the U.S. MNCs in the dollar
devaluations of early 1973.[3] The study pioneered the compilation by the
government of data essential to the analysis of the financial behavior of MNCs.
However, the scope and the design of the investigation still left many important
questions unanswered.

Regardless of the pattern, or lack of pattern, found in the transfer of
funds of these companies, no information was provided on the reasons behind
the behavior of these companies. An understanding of the motivation for these
companies' participation in the exchange markets is essential to assess their
role in these markets. Furthermore, sole reliance on one specific episode in

the exchange markets—the 1973 dollar devaluations—made it difficult to generalize the findings. For example, the control period, early 1972, came soon after a major realignment of currency values in December 1971. Questions could be raised as to how much the instability which preceded this realignment and the credibility of the new currency values affected the behavior of these companies during the control period. To permit generalizations about the role of the MNCs in the exchange markets the period of time studied should be long enough to include several episodes of crisis in the exchange markets.

Plan of this Study

Given this state of the art, an important objective of this study was to gather data which would shed light on two aspects of the exchange-management problem: how managers approached the decision problem and the actual effect of these decisions on international capital flows. This required a two-phase approach: in-depth interviews with financial officers of U.S. MNCs and analysis of quantitative data disaggregated by currency and compiled at the subsidiary level, before corporate consolidation, for a sufficiently long period of time.

I conducted personal interviews with the financial officers of seventy U.S. multinationals. A list of the names of these companies is presented in appendix A. These companies were selected from among the Fortune 500 for their heavy involvement in Europe and Japan. Thus, the companies interviewed are among not only the largest U.S. companies, but also the largest U.S. companies with significant direct investment in developed countries. The exchange fluctuations in the currencies of these countries are the new element in the exchange markets of the 1970s.

Of the companies interviewed, 50 percent considered their export business from the United States to be important. And in 75 percent of these companies the managers considered the degree of intercompany trade to be significant. Exports and intercompany trade provide easy conduits for these companies to move funds around the world. The so-called leads and lags in payments have long been suspected to be among the important forces contributing to exchange crises. The fact that 47 percent of the companies interviewed had a policy of sole ownership of foreign subsidiaries, except where impossible, removes one of the possible impediments to execute transfers of funds in response to exchange-market conditions.[4]

The companies included in this study are certainly capable of moving large amounts of funds from one currency into another. This is the type of company which critics of the multinationals have in mind when they refer to them as the culprit behind the exchange crises. These are also the companies which have had to adapt their policies based on a world where the U.S. dollar had always been considered to be a strong currency, and where exchange problems were traditionally defined as the problem of foreign currencies devaluing against the dollar, to a world where these truisms were no longer valid.

The initial interviews were conducted during the spring of 1974. These interviews had two major parts. The first part gathered background information to identify the areas in the company involved in the generation and management of exposure to exchange risk, that is, those areas involved with the problem of interest in this book. This information facilitated the second portion of the interviews since questions could be then phrased in terms of the specific company situation. This general information also helped to marshall the gathering and coding of quantitative data obtained from these companies. The second part of the interview essentially investigated the procedures used in each company to manage exposure to exchange risk: definition of exposure, systems to gather information, tools used, and actual decision process to cover or not to cover exposures.

A subsample of the seventy companies, consisting of forty companies, were interviewed again during the summer of 1977. The scope of this second set of interviews was narrower than that of the 1974 interviews. In January 1976, Statement No. 8 of the Financial Accounting Standards Board (FASB #8) became effective. This statement established uniform procedures to translate foreign financial statements into dollars. Prior to the use of this statement several translation methods had been accepted. Thus, the major objective of this second set of interviews was to determine the effects, if any, of FASB #8 on the answers gathered during the first round of interviews.

The quantitative data used in this book were obtained from thirty-six U.S. multinationals, a subset of the seventy companies interviewed. These data represent the major European and Japanese subsidiaries for each of the thirty-six companies. Finance subsidiaries, when present, were also included in the sample. This makes a total of approximately 288 subsidiaries.

For each subsidiary of interest, data were collected for separate accounts in each currency.[5] In some companies these data were available from so-called exposure reports submitted by the subsidiaries. In the other companies, the data had to be gathered from regular financial statements submitted by the subsidiary to the company's control department. The period intended to be covered was 1967 to 1974. However, it was not possible to go back to 1967 in every company.

The quantitative data for each company were analyzed from two different standpoints: the behavior for the 1967-1974 period as a whole (analysis of time series) and the behavior during selected periods of turmoil in the exchange markets (cross-sectional analysis). The analysis of the whole period for each company helped to identify what risk attitudes and perceptions of the markets the participating managers had during the period. The analysis of company behavior during periods of crisis in the exchange markets revealed whether and how these companies contributed to these exchange crises.

Organization of the Book

In the following chapters the findings of each of the major parts of the study just described are reported. In chapter 2 the practices revealed during the interviews with the financial officers of the participant companies are discussed. This provides a survey of how these managers approach the various aspects of the exchange-management decision.

After a short review of the conditions in the financial markets during the period 1967-1974 in chapter 3, in chapters 4 and 5 the quantitative data gathered from the companies are analyzed. In chapter 4 a taxonomy of managerial behavior in the exchange-management decision is developed. By pairing different possible risk attitudes and perceptions of the financial markets, a grid of possible exchange policies is created. Then one tests which combination of risk attitude and perception of the markets is best supported by the quantitative data.

In chapter 5 time periods characterized by turmoil in the exchange markets are selected. Then the behavior of the companies is analyzed to determine whether their flow of funds moved in sympathy with market trends. Also, the conduits by which the MNCs participated in the market are examined in this chapter. This sequence of chapters provides a progression in the analysis of the exchange-management decision of U.S. multinationals from the problem as seen by the financial officers of these companies to the impact of their actual behavior during the periods of greatest interest for national economic policy—periods of exchange crises.

Then in the final chapter the findings presented in the earlier chapters are summarized and some conclusions which are expected to be useful to managers and policymakers in the international financial area are drawn.

Notes

1. The only investigation of the behavior of MNCs in the exchange markets available at the time focused on the impact of floating exchange rates on international trade and the hedging of commercial transactions in the forward exchange market. The studies, conducted by Norman S. Fieleke, examined the experiences of the flotation of the Canadian dollar in June 1970 and the flotation of the German mark in 1971. See Norman S. Fieleke, "The Hedging of Commercial Transactions Between U.S. and Canadian Residents: A View from the United States," *Canadian-United States Financial Relationships* (Boston: Federal Reserve Bank of Boston Conference Series, No. 6, 1971), pp. 171-191; and "The 1971 Flotation of the Mark and the Hedging of Commercial Transactions between the United States and Germany: Experiences of Selected U.S. Non-Banking Enterprises," *Journal of International Business Studies*, Spring 1973, pp. 43-59.

Mr. Fieleke's studies did not gather quantitative data, but restricted themselves to analyze the descriptive answers provided by U.S. companies responding to a questionnaire sent to them. The evidence suggested that trade between the United States and the other two countries had not been disrupted by the flotation of the Canadian dollar and the German mark. The impact of floating exchange rates had not affected the ability of these companies to hedge their commercial transactions in the forward-exchange market—partially because they did not often use that market for hedging purposes. A little more of insight into the behavior of MNCs in the exchange markets was revealed by two additional questions asked in the context of the study of the German mark flotation. These additional questions inquired into the methods used by the companies to compute exchange gains and losses resulting from exchange fluctuations and into how they tried to protect themselves from the widely anticipated mark-up valuation. However, the scope of these questions was too narrow to help answer the broader questions which were being raised in 1973 about the whole monetary system and the vast range of MNCs financial practices.

2. Staff report prepared for the use of the Subcommittee on Multinational Corporations of the Committee on Foreign Relations, U.S. Senate, *Multinational Corporations in the Dollar Devaluation Crisis: Report on a Questionnaire* (Washington, D.C.: Government Printing Office, June 1975).

3. However, the researchers did find some evidence that these companies protected themselves against the anticipated devaluation of the dollar by moving funds into stronger currencies and out of weaker ones over the whole period. To accomplish this transfer of funds they did not use the forward market or the banking sector, but instead the companies appeared to rely on shifting the currency composition of liquid assets and debt over a longer period of time.

4. For a complete tabulation of the responses to these questions, see appendix B section I.

5. It should be noted that these data had not been available prior to this study and had to be obtained from the companies directly. In 1977 the U.S. Department of the Treasury began collecting similar data from U.S. multinational companies. See *Treasury Bulletin*, various issues; C. Dirck Keyser, Thomas H.E. Moran, and Maxwell W. Hudgins, Jr., "Exchange Market Behavior of American Firms" (Washington, D.C.: U.S. Department of the Treasury).

2

The Exchange-Management Decision

Financial theory explains how to reach optimal decisions in the management of exposure to exchange risk. An analysis of the company's future cash flows, expected future exchange rates, and current market rates leads to the decision of what the exposure should be in each currency. And if markets are considered to be efficient, in theory the decision does not even matter; over a long period the outcome is the same regardless of the decision made.

Theory, in its pristine simplicity, often ignores many of the realities of corporate life. Thus, the primary objective of the interviews with the financial officers was to understand how these managers approached the exchange-management decision: What factors were important to *them* and how did *they* make tradeoffs among these factors? This understanding, in addition to its intrinsic contribution to the financial literature, was expected to be useful later in gathering and analyzing the quantitative data contributed by each company.

The officers of the seventy companies interviewed were all located at company headquarters. In terms of rank, they often included the senior financial officer in the company as well as some of the staff directly responsible for managing exposure to foreign-exchange risk. The initial interviews were performed during the spring of 1974. A subsample of these seventy companies, consisting of forty companies, were interviewed again during the summer of 1977. The company names are listed in appendix A.

The 1974 interviews had two major parts: a gathering of general background information and a discussion of factors directly relevant to the exchange-management decision. The background information part of the interviews was geared to determining the forms in which foreign-exchange risk affected the particular company. What specific currencies and in what kind of transactions did exposure to exchange risk originate? In this introductory part the organizational areas affected by exchange fluctuations and the areas responsible for controlling these effects were also identified.

The discussion of the exchange-management decision in these companies included questions as to how exposure to exchange risk was defined in the company and how it was reported. After it was established how these managers gathered information about future developments in the exchange markets, the discussion then was focused on the final decision process. Given certain assumed cases, the managers were asked to decide whether to hedge the given exposure. Additional questions inquired on what elements of the decision they placed most importance and how they selected specific hedging tools.

The primary objective of the 1977 interviews was to determine the effects, if any, of FASB #8 on the translation of financial statements (FASB #8 became effective on January 1976). Questions were asked again about the definition of exposure used by the company. But now the question was more specific and addressed what the managers considered to be relevant to calculating exposure, as well as what they used as a basis for hedging decisions. The other questions in these interviews addressed the issue of responsibility and control of various sources of exposure in the company.

The areas covered during the interviews were formalized in a questionnaire, and then the aggregate answers were tabulated. However, the questionnaires were not administered systematically. The interviews were based on a free-flowing discussion of the problem, and the questionnaires were often filled in afterward from the notes taken during the interviews. As a result, not all areas were covered in the same depth in every company. Also, the questionnaire underwent several stages of development before the final one was reached, and some of the questions were not answered by all companies. Sample question-naires with the distribution of answers to each question are presented in appendixes B and C. Appendix B shows the 1974 questionnaire and appendix C the shorter 1977 questionnaire.

The presentation of the information gathered during the interviews is organized in this chapter into three sections describing the major parts of any managerial decision:

1. The setting of objectives
2. The search for alternative solutions
3. The evaluation of alternatives available

Setting Objectives

The Risk-Return Tradeoff

The traditional goal of economists, profit maximization, is not one which managers associate often with the area of foreign-exchange management. Genera-ting profits in foreign exchange is usually seen as "speculative" and therefore outside the scope of proper business management. The statement "we are not in the foreign-exchange business" can be heard frequently as a justification for not pursuing profits in this area. Although anticipating the future price of steel is seen as an obligation of management in the steel industry, anticipation of future exchange rates in a multinational enterprise is considered speculative, something best left to commercial banks.

The most common objective of managing exposure to exchange risk in these companies can be described as reducing exchange risk to some acceptable level—given certain cost constraints. To understand this general position requires a definition of how managers evaluate the various risks and returns involved in the decision, that is, specification of the managers' utility function. But before we can discuss how managers make the tradeoffs necessary to reach a final decision, which is done in the final section of this chapter, we must understand how the relevant variables are defined and measured. We will begin with how exposure to exchange risk is defined in these companies.

The Variable to Be Managed: Exposure

When asked "How do you define exposure to exchange risk in your company?" with few exceptions the managers referred to the exposure reflected in the *translation* of foreign balance sheets. Since the accounting profession allowed several methods of translation for reporting purposes until 1976, some of the accounts considered exposed varied from company to company during the first round of interviews. Also, the treatment of exchange gains and losses for reporting purposes differed among these companies.

A summary of the translation practices followed by these companies before 1976 is presented in table 2-1. It can be seen that the most popular method used by these companies translated all assets, including inventory, and all debt, including long-term debt, at current exchange rates: 63 percent of the companies used this method. Also, more than half of these companies maintained a reserve account where exchange gains and losses were reported directly without appearing first in the income statement.[1]

After further discussion it usually became clear that the initial answer of these managers represented a bit of a simplification; *transaction* types of exposure also were considered at times. (Appendix 2A compares the definitions of translation and transaction exposures.) The two most common cases of exchange transactions which management worried about were remittances to the parent company from subsidiaries (dividends in particular) and specific large transactions denominated in foreign currencies (for example, payments for a plant purchased or built abroad). However, this concern with transaction exposure appears to have been handled on an ad hoc basis in most companies. In only 17 percent of the companies were any records of future exchange transactions maintained. In the other cases there was no reporting system covering these transactions. (See table 2-2.)

As to the time horizon used to analyze balance sheet exposure, table 2-2 shows that in 59 percent of the companies interviewed, management analyzed balance sheet exposure from a report which was often as much as three months behind the period under review. When questioned about the applicability of these exposure figures to the future, management often answered that (1) major changes were incorporated as soon as information was available or (2) the exposure did not change much from quarter to quarter. For the minority of companies following transaction exposure the usual time horizon was less than a year.

Table 2-1

Reporting Practices Used by U.S. Multinationals prior to FASB #8

Translation Rate		Number of	Percentage
Inventory	Long-Term Debt	Companies	of Companies
Companies that had foreign-exchange reserve accounts			
Current	Current	24	34
Historical	Current	7	10
Current	Historical	6	9
Historical	Historical	1	1
		38	54
Companies that did not have foreign-exchange reserve accounts			
Current	Current	20	29
Historical	Current	5	7
Current	Historical	7	10
Historical	Historical	—	—
		32	46
Total		70	100

Source: Data compiled from information in various annual reports of MNCs.

With the advent of FASB #8 in 1976 and the increased experience with floating (and sometimes wildly fluctuating) exchange rates, it appeared desirable to update the information on the definition of exposure used by U.S. multinationals. In the summer of 1977, forty of the original seventy companies were reinterviewed. At that time the question was phrased in two parts: (1) What is the "real economic exposure" to exchange risk in your company? and (2) What measure of exposure do you use when considering hedging alternatives? The answers to these questions are tabulated in tables 2-3 and 2-4.

The term *real economic exposure* was used in this round of interviews to liberate managers from preprogrammed answers and to make them think about the variables which they really consider to be at risk in case of exchange fluctuations. Economic exposure has come to mean different things to different people. However, the term is usually identified as a measure reflecting the "true impact" of exchange rate fluctuations, in contrast to the "paper impact" of translation exposure.

Although the question was posed in terms of economic exposure, accounting or translation exposure was still considered a relevant measure of exposure. Accounting exposure, as measured for purposes of FASB #8, was chosen as a component measure of economic exposure by 86 percent of these companies.

Table 2-2
Variables Measured by the Companies' Exposure Reporting
System in 1974
(*percentage of companies interviewed*)

Historical balance sheet exposure	59
Historical balance sheet updated by changes	3
Forecast balance sheet	14
Future exchange commitments	17
Forecast cash flows per account	5
Forecast profits	2
	100

Note: The figures in this table were computed directly from the notes taken during the interviews with management. The corresponding figures in appendix B, section II.3 are more aggregated. The small discrepancy in numbers between this table and the tabulation in the appendix is due to a few companies which maintained more than one type of reporting system.

However, the concept often had been expanded to include additional variables, particularly inventory and exchange transactions.[2]

The inclusion of inventory as part of accounting exposure can be seen as a reversion to pre-FASB #8 days. The translation methods used by these companies before the adoption of FASB #8 often translated inventory at current exchange rates; 82 percent of the companies interviewed in 1974 followed this practice (see table 2-1). If inventory is translated at current exchange rates and current assets equal current liabilities, there is no exposure to exchange risk under this definition. Needless to say, criticisms of FASB #8 have concentrated heavily on its treatment of the inventory account. (The elimination of reserves for foreign-exchange gains and losses and the treatment of long-term debt also have been the target of severe criticism.)

At the time there was nothing which management could do to modify FASB #8 for external reporting purposes, other than to lobby to have it changed, which it did. However, management could choose to depart from FASB #8 for internal purposes. This is what is reflected by the 59 percent of the companies in the 1977 interviews which considered inventory to be exposed to exchange risk. This is consistent with the 57 percent of the companies who said FASB #8 had had little impact on their actual decisions. (See table 2-5.)[3]

One argument for including inventory among the accounts exposed to exchange risk in the balance sheet is that if FASB #8 translates the liabilities used to finance inventory at current exchange rates, so should the account

Table 2-3
Variables Measured and Considered to Be Part of Economic Exposure by Companies in 1977
(*percentage of companies interviewed*)

	Yes	No	Total
FASB #8 exposure	86	14	100
Inventory	59	41	100
Future profits	8	92	100
Forecast balance sheet	41	59	100
Exchange transactions	55	45	100

Table 2-4
Exposure Definition Most Often Used as a Target for Covering Decisions in 1977
(*percentage of companies interviewed*)

Exchange transactions	60
FASB #8 exposure	20
FASB #8 plus inventory	20
	100

Table 2-5
Impact of FASB #8 on Exposure Management Reported in 1977
(*percentage of companies interviewed*)

Very little impact	57
More attention given to exchange management	20
More inclined to cover exposures	20
Change in financing choice	3
	100

being financed by these liabilities, that is, inventory. (But then why not include fixed assets also?) However, the major practical contribution of this approach is to remove some of the instability in earnings per share produced by the FASB #8 treatment of inventory. When inventory is translated at historical exchange rates, the effect of an exchange rate fluctuation on inventory value is not reflected in the financial statements until the merchandise is sold—usually in the following reporting period. In between, the balance sheet tends to appear in a net liability position for translation purposes. In case of an appreciation in the foreign currency, the company may have to report a foreign-exchange loss because of the balance sheet position, even though it knows that in the following reporting period translated sales will be higher under the new exchange rate. Since reserve accounts for exchange gains and losses are not allowed under FASB #8 (or, in general, in the United States), these inventory gains and losses affect current income directly.

The inclusion of inventory among the accounts considered exposed to exchange risk is also done on economic grounds. For example, in case of a depreciation of the foreign currency, the usual government price controls imposed in such instances, plus marketing considerations, often make it impossible to increase selling prices to compensate for the loss in the exchange rate, at least within the period covered by one inventory turnover cycle.[4]

The concern with inventory as a component of exposure to exchange risk also reflects a lengthening in the time horizon within which exposure is analyzed. While in the 1974 interviews only 14 percent of the companies measured forecast balance sheet exposure in their reporting system (see table 2-2), by 1977 this variable was measured in 41 percent of the companies interviewed (see table 2-3). The number of companies which reported future profits to be exposed to exchange risk, although still modest, also increased from 2 percent in 1974 to 8 percent in 1977.

One of the most significant changes between the 1974 and the 1977 interviews is the role assigned to exchange transactions in the definition of exposure to exchange risk. In 1974 only 17 percent of the companies interviewed maintained a record of exchange transactions planned in the future (see table 2-2). In 1977 this number rose to 55 percent (see table 2-3). More important, when the question was posed in 1977 in terms of what measure of exposure was relevant for hedging decisions, more than half of the respondents, 60 percent, chose transaction exposure as the relevant measure. Only 20 percent of the companies interviewed in 1977 focused on the straight translation definition of exposure (the FASB #8 definition) when considering whether to hedge against exchange risk. The other 20 percent of the companies concentrated on a modified definition of translation exposure which included inventory (see table 2-4).

Not reflected in the figures in these tables is an indirect way for companies to incorporate the extent to which operations can be expected to adjust for exchange rate fluctuations. This is the degree of aggressiveness used in following hedging policies. For example, while using the same definition of exposure, some companies pursued hedging policies more vigorously in cases where price changes could not be expected to compensate for exchange depreciations than when this was not the case. This finer tuning of policies was much more evident during the 1977 interviews than in the earlier ones.

Another measure of the sophistication gained by these managers between 1974 and 1977 is seen in their assessment of tax consequences of exposures to exchange risk. In 1974 only 26 percent of the managers interviewed calculated the tax consequences of exchange exposures. By 1977, a large majority figured taxes into their calculation of exposure.[5] I did not inquire in detail into the methodology used to calculate taxes on exposure. This is a complicated subject, and discrepancies in approaches exist among these managers. However, ignoring taxes does not make them go away. This seems to be the fact grasped by the larger number of managers who in 1977 were willing to incorporate the complexities of tax calculations into their exposure measures.

Searching for Alternative Solutions

Information Systems

The management of exposure to exchange risk requires systems to identify and to calculate the company's exposures and to monitor developments in the exchange markets. The sophistication of each of these control systems varied greatly in the companies interviewed.

Exposure to exchange risk can be compiled at different levels of disaggregation. The statement of exchange exposure can range from providing only a single number for each relevant currency to disclosing the exposure involved in each account for each currency. An itemized disclosure of the components of exposure enables managers to respond with more flexibility. For example, management may want to treat the exposure involved in inventories differently from the exposure in cash items. Also, a disaggregated exposure report conveys information on the extent to which certain tools, such as intercompany accounts, are available to manage exposure.

During the 1974 interviews, 50 percent of the companies had a reporting system which disaggregated exposure by currency and account, and in 9 percent of the companies the reporting system provided net exposure by currency without any disaggregation. The other 41 percent did not have any formalized foreign-exchange reports.[6] In these cases the information on exposure to exchange risk was limited to what could be obtained from the regular financial statements submitted by the foreign units to the control department. The definition of exposure was constrained to the accounting definition, and the estimate of exposure was derived after assuming all the balance sheet accounts were in local currency, except as might have been noted on footnotes to the statements. The exposure figure for the given reporting unit was then computed as the net of the balance sheet accounts translated at current exchange rates. For companies where foreign subsidiaries are self-contained within their countries of operation, this method provides a reasonable approximation of historical translation exposures. However, where this assumption is not valid, this method provides inaccurate exposure figures at best, and misleading ones at worst.

Also, to the extent that transaction exposure is deemed important or that translation exposure may change from one reporting period to the next, current balance sheet figures do not provide relevant information. The 59 percent of the companies which in table 2-2 were reported to consider historical balance sheet exposures, usually three months behind, include all the companies which did not have a specialized exposure reporting system and depended on other financial reports to compute exposure to exchange risk.

The companies' systems to monitor exchange-market developments, the other major piece of information necessary to the exchange-management decision, were also varied. No company relied on a single source. Listed in decreasing order of frequency of response, the sources of forecast-exchange-rate movements were commercial banks' traders and lending officers, 51 percent; specialized foreign-exchange advisory services, 38 percent; information provided by foreign subsidiaries, 27 percent; in-house economic department, 27 percent; and unspecified sources, 31 percent. (Percentages do not add to 100 because multiple responses were possible for each company.) The most typical forecasting horizon was one year, although forecasts were often revised monthly. Except for two companies which had a formal in-house simulation model, foreign-exchange forecasts were the result of management consensus reached after a review of the evidence available.[7]

Responsibility and Control

Organization theory indicates that business decisions are heavily influenced by the fact that various levels of the organization are involved in the decision. Thus, it appeared desirable to establish what levels of the organization of the companies interviewed were involved in the management of exposure to exchange risk. This line of questioning was narrowed to determining the levels of the company that made decisions capable of generating exposures to exchange risk and the levels of the company responsible for controlling these exposures. Because our interviews were conducted with only the financial officers of these companies, the primary objective of these questions was to determine how much responsibility and control of exposure rested in the finance department, and how much elsewhere in the company.

We can think of two major areas of decision making where exposure to exchange risk can be generated. First, the basic operations of the company as represented by marketing and production decisions may involve foreign currencies. Second, the financing of these operations may or may not be done in the same currency as the currency of operations. Transaction and translation exposures are generated by both types of decisions.

The responsibility and the control of operations clearly rest with marketing and production personnel. The decision of whether to bill in local currency or in foreign currency is essentially a marketing decision. The decision of whether to manufacture abroad is a production decision. The finance department may or may not be consulted on the exposure implications of these decisions, but rarely would finance considerations dictate the outcome of these decisions, nor would the treasury department be held responsible for them. The responsibility and the control of the financing decision, on the other hand, are not so clearly defined. They can be assigned to either the operating units or the finance department; so can the associated responsibility for the translation and transaction exposures generated.

During both the 1974 and the 1977 interviews, questions were asked about what level in the company was responsible for raising funds. The responsibility for raising long-term funds, almost without exception, was with the finance department of the company. The responsibility for short-term funds, on the other hand, was as often delegated to the foreign subsidiaries as kept with the finance department. Table 2-6 shows how the respondents in each interview assigned the responsibility for raising short-term funds.

Between 1974 and 1977 the responsibility for raising short-term funds was redistributed in these companies. In 1974 about half of the respondents had their subsidiaries responsible for raising short-term funds within guidelines provided by the parent company. By 1977 only 21 percent of the companies interviewed followed this pattern. The decrease in importance of this approach to financing had been taken up by two opposite trends: greater centralization at headquarters and greater freedom for the subsidiaries. In 1974 the parent company was directly involved in providing the needed funds in 36 percent of the companies interviewed. By 1977 the percentage of companies reporting centralized short-term financing had increased to 51 percent. Simultaneously, while only 7 percent of the companies interviewed allowed their subsidiaries to raise short-term funds without any guidelines provided by the parent

Table 2-6
Responsibility for Raising Short-Term Funds in U.S. Multinationals,
1974 and 1977
(*percentage of companies interviewed*)

	1974	1977
Subsidiary		
With guidelines from parent	51	21
Without guidelines from parent	7	28
	58	49
Parent's financial staff	36	51
Joint: Subsidiary presents proposals, final decision taken by parent	6	—
	100	100

company, in 1977 28 percent did so. The use of rules in the form of guidelines appears to have lost favor with these companies in the intervening period. Instead, a larger number of companies preferred to either centralize the financial decision at headquarters or to give greater freedom to the subsidiaries. The rapidly changing environment may help explain this trend.

Although the financing decision was often centralized at the level of the parent company, foreign subsidiaries were often held accountable for the outcomes of financing decisions. During the 1974 interviews the question of responsibility for foreign-exchange risk was not included explicitly in the questionnaire, although the subject was often discussed. However, in the 1977 interviews the question was raised directly. The managers interviewed were asked about the level in the financial statements for which subsidiaries were held responsible. The answers to this question are tabulated in table 2-7.

The line in the income statement on which the subsidiaries' evaluations are based determines for how much of the effects of financing decisions and the effects of the local currency fluctuations against the dollar the subsidiaries are held accountable. In terms of local currency, the subsidiaries may be evaluated on the basis of operating profits or profits after interest and taxes. Operating profits exclude interest charges and therefore the cost of financing decisions. Both operating profits and profits after taxes in local currency exclude the changes in value of the local currency against the dollar reflected in the translation of the financial statements. The fluctuations of the local currency against the dollar, which a foreign subsidiary would consider totally outside its control, are included to some extent when the evaluation is based on dollar figures. Dollar operating profits include only the translation of this item into dollars. However, dollar profits after interest and taxes and after translation of the balance sheet involve the full impact of financing decisions, including the changes in value of the total liabilities outstanding.

Table 2-7
Most Comprehensive Financial Variable Used in Evaluating Foreign Subsidiaries in 1977
(*percentage of companies interviewed*)

Local currency operating profits before interest and taxes	18
Local currency profits after taxes	21
Dollar operating profits before interest and taxes	11
Dollar profits before taxes, but after balance sheet translation	9
Dollar profits after taxes, excluding balance sheet translation	3
Dollar profits after taxes, including balance sheet translation	32
Dollar profits after taxes, including and excluding balance sheet translation	6
	100

Table 2-7 shows that only 18 percent of the companies restricted the evaluation of foreign subsidiaries to purely operational matters; that is, they were evaluated on the basis of local currency operating profits before interest and taxes. The effects of both translation of financial statements into dollars and financing were totally excluded from the evaluation of these subsidiaries. In another 21 percent of the companies, subsidiaries were evaluated in terms of local currency profits after taxes. In these cases interest charges were included in the evaluation, but the effects of translation were excluded. To the extent that the financing decision was delegated to the foreign subsidiaries, these affiliates were evaluated on items which were under their control. But in 41 percent of the companies the subsidiaries were evaluated in terms of profits before or after taxes, but after financing charges and translation of the balance sheet. That is, the effects of exchange fluctuations of their currency against the dollar (which were reflected in the translation of their financial statements) and the effects of financing decisions (which often were made by the parent company) were included in the evaluation of these subsidiaries. The effects of translation were limited for the 11 percent which were evaluated in terms of dollar profits before interest and taxes. In these cases only the translation of operating profits was added to the basic responsibilities of the operating personnel.

It is generally accepted that managers should be evaluated only in terms of things which are under their control. If this is the case, a number of the companies interviewed followed practices which could be a source of conflict between the foreign subsidiaries and the parent company. For example, with the company's treasury department having the responsibility for raising the funds needed for operations by the foreign subsidiaries, those subsidiaries evaluated in terms of profits after taxes had their evaluation affected by interest charges which they did not negotiate. Depending on whether they were evaluated on dollar or local currency profits and on whether the debt was denominated in dollar or local currency, they may have run an additional exchange risk for which they did not bargain. The inclusion of the translation of the balance sheet in the evaluation could exacerbate this problem when financing was not done in the local currency. In this case the balance sheet exposure was larger than if financing had been done in the local currency. The changes in the value of this exposure in dollars affected the subsidiaries' bottom line every reporting period that this translation effect was included.[9]

Managers confronted with these examples of conflict responded that the treasury department was better able to see the company as a whole than each separate subsidiary and that subsidiaries could not ignore the fact that they belonged to a U.S. company which reported consolidated financial statements in dollar terms, and they should be so evaluated. In practice, many of these decisions which affect the evaluation of the subsidiary were made in consultation with the subsidiary, even though the final responsibility for the decision may have rested with the parent company. Presumably the concerns of the operating managers were raised during the consultation, and hopefully taken into account in the final decision by the parent company. That is, informal decision mechanisms may solve the conflicts which the official system incorporates. Given that the interviews were limited to the financial office, no further inquiry was carried in this area.

Thus, we can think of two major functional sources of exposure to exchange risk: operations and financing. Responsibility and control of exposure derived from operations rest in the hands of the same individuals—line management. Responsibility and control of the exposure involved in financing decisions did not always coincide in the same individuals in the companies interviewed. Often the managers of the subsidiaries were held responsible for these decisions while the control of the decisions remained with the parent company's financial staff. Conflict or not, the treasury department often had final control over a large source of the company's exposure to exchange risk—financing. So, they also had control over financing as a tool to modify exposures. This area is discussed in the following section.

After operational and financing decisions are made and their exchange exposure implications accepted by the parties held accountable for them, management of the exposure thus created must continue. Responsibility and control of this exposure were located almost exclusively with the financial department of the company. This is the exposure to which the managers interviewed referred during our discussions.

Exposure-Management Tools

Before the financial office can reach a decision as to whether to hedge an exposure, hedging tools must be identified and evaluated. During the interviews four hedging tools were identified, and the managers were asked to rank the tools according to the frequency with which they used them. The following tools were listed:

1. Leads and lags in intercompany payments. (Remit funds in advance from countries with weak currencies and delay the remittance of funds from countries with strong currencies.)
2. Money market transactions. (Increase borrowings in weak currencies and investments in strong currencies.)
3. Cover the exposure in the forward-exchange market.
4. Alter the terms of trade in receivables and payables (increase payables and decrease receivables in weak currencies and do the opposite in strong currencies) and lead or lag remittances as in (1).

Table 2-8 shows that leads and lags, together with money market transactions, were the two most popular tools used in altering exposures. The tool used next most frequently involved the forward market. Although most companies appeared to show little hesitation to use the first two tools, they were much more careful in resorting to the forward-exchange market.[10] Indeed, many companies considered the use of this market speculative and something to be done only as a measure of last resort. Finally, the alteration of terms of trade with third parties was a measure which most companies generally avoided. Interfering with the marketing and production functions of the business was considered to be outside the scope of the exposure-management function in most cases.

Companies' large inclination to consider money market instruments, as well as leading and lagging intercompany payments, can be seen as an extension of the control of the parent company over all financing decisions discussed earlier. Borrowing in one currency and investing in another is parallel to providing short-term funds to subsidiaries. A similar situation occurs with leading and lagging payments. To the extent that a prepayment is made from a subsidiary located in a weak currency, an alternative source of funds must be found. This source usually is obtained by borrowing local funds. Similarly, as subsidiaries located in countries with strong currencies delay making remittances to other subsidiaries or to the parent company, a use for those funds must be found. This use usually will be investment of the funds within the country.

In view of these companies' willingness to tap the money market to hedge undesirable exposures to exchange risk, their reluctance to use the forward exchange market for the same purpose appears peculiar. The one-to-one relationship between interest rate differentials in the money market and forward rate premiums or discounts in the exchange market is well known.[11] In theory,

Table 2-8
Ranking of Various Tools Used in Managing Exchange Exposure in U.S. Multinationals
(*tool most used = 1; tool least used = 4*)

	Average Rank of Tool among Companies Interviewed
Lead-lag of intercompany accounts (Remit in advance funds from weak-currency country, delay remittance of funds from strong-currency country.)	1.68
Money market with transfer of funds (Borrow weak currency and invest in strong currency.)	1.87
Forward-exchange market	2.49
Terms of trade in receivables and payables with third parties	3.74

the manager should be indifferent to using the money market or the forward-exchange market to accomplish a given hedging operation. If anything, the manager should find the money market route to be more expensive to the extent that commercial banks charge a premium on money market transactions to cover the credit risk which is involved on a loan, but not on a forward-exchange contract. In addition, loans and investments resulting from money market transactions are reported on the main body of the balance sheet; forward exchange contracts are reported in footnotes, if at all. That is, money market hedges affect some of the usual financial ratios computed from balance sheet figures, while forward contracts do not. However, in the income statement the interest cost of money market hedges is reported together with other interest expenses while any gain or loss on a forward-exchange contract is reported as an exchange gain or loss. Foreign-exchange gains and losses are considered by many analysts to have a higher visibility than interest cost.

In spite of the indifference to money market hedges and forward contract hedges postulated by theory, or the likely practical superiority of forward contracts, most of the managers interviewed had a very clear preference for money market transactions over forward-exchange contracts. This preference could be justified in cases where the thin exchange market for the currency, plus the existence of government exchange controls, makes the forward rates depart from the close relationship to money market rates anticipated by theory. In these cases the money market route to hedging, if accessible, is truly superior to the forward-exchange market. This is the case with the currencies of most developing countries. In the other cases, however, lack of familiarity with the exchange markets and reluctance to report any exchange gain or loss appear to be the best explanations for management's unwillingness to use forward-exchange contracts for hedging purposes. Somehow forward contracts are perceived as signs of speculation, while loans and investments evidence sound financial management practices.

Finally, the relationships of the firm with its suppliers and its customers usually were regarded as the domain of the operating manager, and therefore an area where the financial officer should not interfere. Thus, the unwillingness of these managers to interfere with regular business operations to change the company's exposure to exchange risk is predictable. Under this general policy, however, cases were found where companies had resorted to this route under extreme circumstances. Also, gradations in the closeness with which accounts receivable were scrutinized could be found as circumstances in a given currency changed.

Evaluating Alternatives

The last step in a decision process is to evaluate alternatives and to select the most desirable one. In the section "Setting Objectives," further discussion of these managers' objective of reducing exchange risk to acceptable levels was postponed until we had discussed how these managers measured and evaluated the risks and returns involved in the exchange-management decision. We have discussed how these managers gather information and measure the relevant variables; now we turn to the final choice: to hedge or not to hedge.

A Generalized Analysis

In order to decide whether to hedge an exposure to exchange risk, management must compare the expected exchange gains or losses from leaving the exposure uncovered with the costs of covering it.[12] The relevant figures in this comparison are the rates available for hedging the exposure (forward exchange premium/discount, or interest rate differentials) and the anticipated future spot rate.

If the spot exchange rate fluctuates while an exposure exists, an exchange gain or loss will occur. If we assume a positive exposure, if the exchange rate appreciates, there will be a gain; if the exchange rate depreciates, there will be a loss. However, this gain or loss will not be known until the spot rate actually moves. Leaving the position open exposes the company to the risk of possible exchange losses, although gains also may occur.

If management chooses to hedge the exposure to exchange risk, such as by entering in a forward-exchange contract, management knows in advance the exchange rate at which the exposure will be converted eventually, that is, the forward-exchange rate. The risks involved in the open position are eliminated. However, other risks are created. It will not be until the eventual future spot rate is known with certainty that the manager will be able to assert the opportunity cost of the hedging decision.

More specifically, to decide whether to hedge an exposure to exchange risk, managers examine this relationship:

$$\left(\begin{array}{c} \text{Forward} \\ \text{rate} \end{array} - \begin{array}{c} \text{Current} \\ \text{spot rate} \end{array} \right) \gtreqless \left(\begin{array}{c} \text{Expected future} \\ \text{spot rate} \end{array} - \begin{array}{c} \text{Current} \\ \text{spot rate} \end{array} \right)$$

which is the same as

$$\left(\begin{array}{c} \text{Exchange gain (loss)} \\ \text{if exposure is covered} \end{array} \right) \gtreqless \left(\begin{array}{c} \text{Expected exchange gain (loss)} \\ \text{if exposure is } not \text{ covered} \end{array} \right)$$

Depending on the sign of this inequality, managers can select the optimum strategy. But notice that the degree of uncertainty is not the same on both terms of this relationship. For a single transaction the exchange gain (loss) if the exposure is covered is known from the beginning. The actual gain (loss) if the exposure is *not* covered will not be known until the exposure is converted at the end of the period. At the time of the hedging decision, the expected future spot rate is only an average of possible future spot rates which may fluctuate over a wide range.

If it were possible to define the relationship between the forward rate and the expected future spot rate, then the above relationship could become an equality. This would be the case if the forward rate were to incorporate properly the expectations for future changes in the spot rate. Then the forward rate equals the expected future spot rate in the formulation above, and the hedging loss (gain) because of the forward-rate discount (premium) will equal the expected loss (gain) if the exposure were left uncovered. The value of the exposure would be the same whether or not it is covered.

But even in markets where the forward rate can be presumed to incorporate all information available about future developments in the spot rate (the so-called efficient markets), the forward rate cannot be expected to be an accurate predictor of the spot rate. The expected spot rate in the formulation above still is uncertain for *specific* transactions. However, in this market the forward rate can be expected to predict the spot rate in terms of *averages*: The forward rate equals the average of all possible spot rates weighed by the probability of their occurrence. Over a long period the errors made by the predictions embedded in the forward rate should tend to cancel. The forward rate will overestimate the future spot rate as often as it will underestimate it. In this market, it still would be difficult to anticipate whether it would be better to hedge a specific exposure. But if *many* such exposures were analyzed, then for all of them combined it would make no difference whether they were covered. The aggregate exchange gains (losses) from covering the exposures would approximate the aggregate exchange gains (losses) which would have been realized if the exposures had not been covered.[13]

With governments of major currencies allowing exchange rates to fluctuate more freely since 1973, these rates have come to reflect the market's assessments more accurately. In a market of flexible exchange rates, the forward rate reflects market expectations better than in a system of fixed rates maintained through government intervention. With floating rates the comparison of forward discounts (premiums) with expected changes in the spot rate described above should leave management often indifferent as to whether to cover an exposure. However, this would be the case only if management based its decisions exclusively on *expected values*. Conversations with management indicated this may not be the case.

The Managers' Analysis

During the interviews the risk aversion of several managers manifested in a very strong distaste for exchange losses, particularly large ones. For some of these managers, avoiding exchange losses appeared to be the primary objective of the exchange-management function. Hedging costs and forgone exchange gains played only a secondary role in those cases. These managers based their decision not on *simple expected values*, but on *reweighted expected values* where possible exchange losses carried a heavier weight than exchange gains.

To test how managers' aversion to reporting exchange losses affects their hedging decisions, if at all, I first provided assumptions where managers who base their decision on simple expected values would be indifferent as to whether to cover an exposure. All managers were told, and they agreed, that in the post-1973 world of floating exchange rates it was virtually impossible to forecast exchange-rate movements accurately. Then they were asked to assume, for the purposes of the questions, that the forward rate was the best forecast available of the future spot rate. Several of the managers argued with this assumption, but they went along with it. Essentially, I asked these managers to assume that the exchange market was an efficient market. As described earlier, under these conditions the expected value of exposures is the same whether covered or not. However, the managers were not told explicitly of this implication.

Given the general description of the nature of the exchange market, I then provided additional information affecting the magnitude of possible reported exchange losses. Two devices were used: (1) The average expected spot rate, represented by the forward-exchange rate, was varied so that if this rate materialized, the firm would report exchange losses, no exchange gains or losses, or exchange gains, depending on the case. (2) The maximum exchange fluctuations possible around the expected rate were assumed to be of the same magnitude on each side of the expected rate (a symmetrical distribution) in some cases, and in other cases they were larger on one side than on the other (an asymmetrical distribution). With a symmetrical distribution the possible maximum exchange loss would be the same as the maximum gain; with an asymmetrical distribution this would not be the case.

For managers who based their decision on simple expected values, without reweighing the possible rates according to their personal aversions, the additional market information provided should not have had any effect. As described above, they would be indifferent as to whether to cover an exposure. However, for those managers who were concerned more with avoiding exchange losses than with minimizing hedging costs, there would be a greater interest in covering the exposures when the average expected rate involved an exchange loss than when an exchange gain was expected. And the interest in covering an exposure would increase as the magnitude of the possible maximum exchange loss increased relative to the possible maximum exchange gain—even though the expected value of the exposure remained the same whether covered or uncovered.[14]

In the interest of brevity during the interviews, four cases were selected from the possible combinations of the factors just discussed:

1. An expected exchange loss with a distribution of future spot rates skewed to the left

2. An expected exchange loss with a symmetrical distribution of future spot rates
3. An expectation of zero exchange gain/loss with a symmetrical distribution of future spot rates
4. An expected exchange gain with a distribution of future spot rates skewed to the right

The specification of the shape of the distributions of future spot rates, like the assumption of an efficient exchange market, was done indirectly during the interviews. For example, to indicate a distribution of future spot rates skewed to the left, but with a depreciated rate as an expected value, the following type of statement was made: "Assume that a depreciation of around 5 percent is expected (the currency in question is selling at a 5 percent discount in the forward exchange market). If there is a depreciation, it could be as large as 20 percent, although a devaluation of this magnitude is not very likely. An appreciation, if it occurred, would not be much higher than 5 percent." The shape of the distribution of possible changes in the spot rate in this case is presented in figure 2-1.

A tabulation of the answers to the various cases obtained during the interviews is presented in table 2-9. In spite of assuming conditions which could

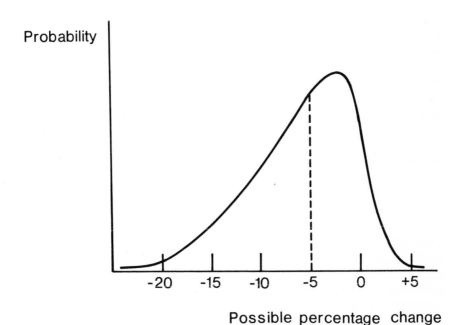

Figure 2-1. Asymmetrical Density Function, Change in Rates.

Table 2-9
Exposure-Management Decisions under Alternative Market Scenarios
(*percentage of companies interviewed*)

Assumptions Common to All Cases:

1. *Company has a large net positive exposure in the given currency.*
2. *The forward rate is considered an unbiased predictor of the future spot rate.*

Case 1:   Spot rate is expected to *depreciate* on average; that is, an exchange *loss* is expected.

Maximum possible depreciation of spot rate is larger than maximum possible appreciation.

Will leave position open	7
Will bring position to zero	82
Will bring position to be negative	11
	100

Case 2:   Spot rate is expected to *depreciate* on average; that is, an exchange *loss* is expected.

Maximum possible depreciation of spot rate equals maximum possible appreciation.

Will leave position open	40
Will bring position to zero	60
	100

Case 3:   Spot rate is expected to remain *constant* on average; no exchange gain or loss is expected.

Maximum possible depreciation of spot rate equals maximum possible appreciation.

Will leave position open	82
Will bring position to zero	18
	100

Case 4:   Spot rate is expected to *appreciate* on average; that is, an exchange *gain* is expected.

Maximum possible appreciation of spot rate is larger than maximum possible depreciation.

Will leave position open	42
Will bring position to zero	29
Will bring position to be even more positive	29
	100

---

prove the hedging decision to be a trivial one—the value of the exposures over a period is the same whether hedged or not—these managers were *not* indifferent to the additional market information provided. If these managers had based their decisions on the average expected rates, they would have covered the exposures as often as not. In addition, the responses to the different cases would not have differed. As table 2-9 shows, this is not the case. The number of managers who chose to cover or not to cover is far from 50 percent in every case. Also there seems to be a trend in the responses. The number of managers who chose to cover the exposure declines from case 1 to case 4.

In the first case an exchange loss was expected, and the loss could be very large, much larger than any possible exchange gain. Under these conditions, most managers (82 percent of the respondents) wanted to engage in hedging operations to bring the initial exposure to zero. Only 7 percent of the managers interviewed chose to leave the position open under these conditions. However, 11 percent were willing to convert the initial positive exposure into a negative one in order to profit from the expected exchange depreciation.

In the second case, as in case 1, an exchange loss was still expected on average. However, unlike in case 1, in case 2 there was symmetry between the maximum possible movement of the exchange rate on either side of the expected value. Under these conditions, the percentage of managers who chose to close the position in case 2 went down to 60 percent from 82 percent in case 1.

In case 3, the average expectation was no exchange gain or loss. In addition, the probability of extreme losses occurring was the same as for gains of the same magnitude—a symmetrical distribution. The change from an expected exchange loss in case 2 to no gain or loss expected in case 3 reduced the proportion of managers who wanted to hedge the exchange position further. Now only 18 percent of the managers interviewed rushed to cover the position; the remaining 82 percent left it open.

Finally, in case 4 an exchange gain was expected. In addition, the assumed distribution of future spot rates was the mirror image of the one in case 1; the maximum possible movement in the exchange rate was higher on the appreciation than on the depreciation side, the opposite of case 1. These conditions brought the percentage of managers wanting to close the exposure down to 29 percent, in contrast to 82 percent in case 1. In case 4, 42 percent of the managers were willing to leave the position open and 29 percent were willing to increase the size of the positive exposure to benefit from the expected appreciation. In case 1, with an expected exchange loss, only 7 percent left it open and only 11 percent volunteered to adjust the position to benefit from an exchange depreciation.

The responses tabulated in table 2-9 show clearly that the *managers interviewed were more inclined to cover an exposure to exchange risk when an exchange loss was the expected outcome than when no change in the spot rate or an exchange gain were expected. This aversion to reporting exchange losses was magnified when large exchange losses were possible.* Although under the assumed conditions the expected exchange gain or loss would have been the same whether the exposure was covered or not, the sign of the expected value and the magnitude of the maximum possible loss affected the decision made.

Because we assumed that the forward rate was the best forecaster of the future spot rate available, the formulation presented earlier in the generalized analysis should have provided on average an equality as follows:

$$\frac{\text{Forward}}{\text{rate}} - \frac{\text{Current}}{\text{spot rate}} = \frac{\text{Expected future}}{\text{spot rate}} - \frac{\text{Current}}{\text{spot rate}}$$

which is the same as

$$\frac{\text{Exchange gain (loss)}}{\text{if exposure is covered}} = \frac{\text{Expected exchange gain (loss)}}{\text{if exposure is } not \text{ covered}}$$

Instead, it appears these managers saw an inequality which favored a specific course of action as follows. When an exchange loss was expected,

$$\frac{\text{Exchange loss if}}{\text{exposure is covered}} < \frac{\text{Expected exchange loss if}}{\text{exposure is } not \text{ covered}}$$

so the exposure was covered. And when an exchange gain was expected,

$$\frac{\text{Exchange gain if}}{\text{exposure is covered}} < \frac{\text{Expected exchange gain if}}{\text{exposure is } not \text{ covered}}$$

so the exposure was left open, not covered.

Given the initial assumptions, these inequalities are possible only if these managers assigned larger weights to losses than to gains when the positions were left open. The left side of these formulations is known with certainty. However, the expected future spot rate covers a range of possible values. Some of these produce exchange gains; others, exchange losses. If managers believe that $1 of possible exchange losses carries a heavier weight than $1 of possible exchange gains, even if the dollar amount of expected exchange gains and expected exchange losses is the same, the aggregate weighted according to the manager's preferences will not be zero, but a net loss. Therefore, these managers were more inclined to cover exposures when the expected outcome involved an exchange loss, as in case 1, than when exchange gains were expected, as in case 4.

If, in addition to the weighing process just described, the difference between the weight assigned to a possible gain and that assigned to a possible loss increases with the magnitude of the possible loss, then the above inequalities become even bigger when large extreme values for future spot rates can be expected. This is consistent with the results presented in table 2-9. In cases 1 and 2 an exchange loss was expected; however, an extremely large loss was possible only in case 1. As a result, 82 percent of the managers chose to cover the exposure in case 1, versus 60 percent in case 2. But when the extreme possible values represented an exchange gain, as in case 4, only 29 percent chose to cover the exposure.

Summary

The dominant objective of managing exchange risk for the managers interviewed is to minimize risk, not to maximize profits. However, this risk is measured not just by the standard deviation of the expected results. These managers' perception of risk is heavily colored by the nature of the outcome to be reported in the financial statements of the company.

The primary measure of exposure to exchange risk analyzed by these managers is exposure as defined for effects of translating foreign financial statements into dollars. Although since 1973 there has been an increasing emphasis on the exposure involved in exchange transactions, 86 percent of the managers interviewed in 1977 still considered balance sheet exposure at least an important component of exposure.

The system to gather information about the magnitude of exposures in these companies ranged from detailed reports where exposures in each currency were disaggregated by major account by each reporting unit to the total absence of any specialized exposure report. In the latter case exposure figures were derived from standard reports submitted to the controller's office for financial reporting with inaccuracies often creeping in. During the 1974 interviews only half these large companies had a formal foreign-exchange reporting system. By 1977, although not qualified, the number of respondents who appeared to have a more formalized reporting system had increased. The degree of sophistication in approaching the problem had increased with the experience in the intervening years of floating exchange rates.

By and large, the most popular source of forecasts of exchange-market development was commercial banks in their traditional relations with business as lending officers and exchange traders. Specialized advisory services in banks and elsewhere also enjoyed a relatively large popularity with these companies.

The exposures to exchange risk for which these managers were responsible almost exclusively referred to the exposure existing after operational and financing decisions were made. Presumably exchange considerations also entered in the earlier decisions; however, the degree to which the financial officers were responsible for these decisions was different. They were not responsible nor held accountable for regular operational decisions. However, they often were responsible for providing short-term funds for foreign operations, although foreign units often were held accountable for the results of these financing decisions. This control over financing operations gave additional tools to these managers not only to modify undesirable exposures, but also to position the company in the path of desirable ones.

When choosing a hedging tool, these managers overwhelmingly preferred a money market instrument instead of a forward-exchange contract. The fact that the borrowing and investment associated with money market hedges can be submerged into the regular business activities of this nature appears to have influenced these managers to favor this avenue over forward-exchange contracts.

Gains and losses on exchange contracts are identified separately in the income statement as exchange gains or losses—not as interest costs.

Finally, managers' risk aversion manifested in a decision process which placed a heavier weight on possible outcomes involving an exchange loss than on outcomes involving exchange gains. Given situations where a decision based on simple expected values would have left the manager indifferent as to whether to hedge an exposure, these managers usually chose to hedge it whenever the expected average represented an exchange loss—despite the fact that anticipation was already reflected in the forward rate. When exchange gains were likely to result, most managers were willing to leave their exposures open and to forgo the opportunity of locking in the gain already reflected on the forward rate.

Notes

1. A summary of the accounting practices used in the translation of balance sheets of these companies before the adoption of the Financial Accounting Standards Boards Statement No. 8 is presented in Rita M. Rodriguez, "FASB No. 8: What Has It Done for US?" *Financial Analysts Journal,* March/April 1977, pp. 40-48.

2. For a description of the translation procedures specified by FASB #8 see appendix 2A. Statement No. 8 of the Financial Accounting Standards Board (FASB #8) specifies the following translation practice:

Accounts Translated at:

Current Exchange Rates	*Historical Exchange Rates*
Cash	Inventory at cost
Accounts receivable	Fixed assets
Inventory at market	
Short-term liabilities	
Long-term liabilities	

Given that the inventory account is usually measured at cost, inventory values are translated at historical exchange rates in most cases. In the definition of exposure where only accounts translated at current exchange rates are considered exposed to exchange risk, inventory as translated under FASB #8 is usually *not* exposed.

For a detailed discussion of the translation of the inventory account see Financial Accounting Standards Board, *Statement of Financial Accounting Standards No. 8* (Stamford, Connecticut, October 1975).

3. The relatively small impact of FASB #8 on exchange-management decisions reported in this book is in contrast to the overwhelming antipathy FASB #8 has elicited from management in general. Management's dislike for FASB #8 has been covered amply by the press. The intensity of such criticisms

has been such that in 1979 the Financial Accounting Standards Board was in the process of modifying FASB #8. A study found that 71 percent of the respondents to a questionnaire found FASB #8 worse than the translation method the companies previously used. (Marjorie T. Stanley and Stanley B. Block, "Response by United States Financial Managers to Financial Accounting Standard No. 8," *Journal of International Business Studies*, Fall 1978, pp. 89-99.) This study also found that 23 percent of the respondents had taken actions to reduce accounting exposure which resulted in an increase in economic exposure. This is consistent with the 20 percent of the companies studied in this book who answered they were more inclined to cover exposures after FASB #8 and the 3 percent who reported a change in financing choice.

4. For a discussion of a comprehensive measure of economic exposure see Rita M. Rodriguez, "Measuring and Controlling Multinationals' Exchange Risk," *Financial Analysts Journal*, November/December 1979, pp. 49-55.

5. See appendix B, section II.4.

6. See appendix B, section II.2.

7. See appendix B, section III, questions 1 to 4. For an evaluation of various forecasting techniques see Stephen H. Goodman, "Foreign Exchange Rate Forecasting Techniques: Implications for Business and Policy," *Journal of Finance*, May 1979, pp. 415-427.

8. This may represent a more advanced step in the evolution of the financial function discussed by Robbins and Stobaugh. See Sidney M. Robbins and Robert B. Stobaugh, *Money in the Multinational Enterprise* (New York: Basic Books, 1973), pp. 37-47.

9. This kind of conflict was also identified by Robbins and Stobaugh, *Money in the Multinational Enterprise*, pp. 154-160.

10. Using the U.S. Treasury data on nonbank exchange positions for the period March 1975 to March 1978, Norman S. Fieleke also concludes that U.S. companies do not use the forward-exchange market very much to cover their balance sheet exchange positions. See Norman S. Fieleke, "Foreign-Currency Positioning by U.S. Firms: Some New Evidence," June 1979 (unpublished manuscript). Fieleke found similar results when he studied the experiences of the flotation of the Canadian dollar in 1970 and the German mark in 1971. "The Hedging of Commercial Transactions between U.S. and Canadian Residents: A View from the United States," *Canadian-United States Financial Relationships* (Boston: Federal Reserve Bank of Boston Conference Series, No. 6, 1971) pp. 175-176; and "The 1971 Flotation of the Mark and the Hedging of Commercial Transactions between the United States and Germany: Experiences of Selected U.S. Non-Banking Enterprises," *Journal of International Business Studies*, Spring 1973, pp. 47-48.

11. For example, see Rita M. Rodriguez and E. Eugene Carter, *International Financial Management*, 2d ed. (Englewood Cliffs, N.J.: Prentice Hall, 1979), pp. 146-149.

12. In this book the terms *hedging* and *covering* an exchange exposure are used interchangeably.

13. For further discussion of the nature of foreign-exchange markets and the hedging decision, see Rodriguez and Carter, *International Financial Management*, chapters 5 and 7.

14. Asymmetrical distributions can result from true market assessments or from the overcautious manager's imagination. Some support for real market assessments which are skewed can be found in many of the forecasts of ranges of future spot rates provided to managers by forecasting services. There is some evidence that when the forecasting errors implicit in the forward rate are pooled for many periods, these errors tend to fall on a normal distribution. The forward rate overestimates the spot rate as often as it underestimates it. However, there is also evidence that in the cases of *large* changes in the spot rate, the forward rate tends to underestimate the magnitude of the change. Managers may incorporate this fact into their analysis by systematically assigning some finite probability to extremely undesirable events—even if most market analysts at the time find such a fluctuation improbable. The stability which a system of flexible exchange rates had promised has not materialized.

Appendix 2A
Traditional Exposure
Measures Compared

The purpose of measuring exposure to exchange risk is to identify the amount at stake in case of an exchange fluctuation. Once this amount has been determined, then it is possible to estimate the magnitude of the gain or loss which will accompany any specific movement in exchange rates.

The two traditional exposure measures are *translation* and *transaction* exposures. This appendix will discuss the rationale behind each of these measures plus a variant of translation exposure. It will be shown that each of the exposure measures currently in use focuses on a different concept of what is at risk. In fact, each of these definitions of exposure pursues a different objective.

The Accountants' Measure: Translation Exposure

The preparation of consolidated financial statements for a multinational company requires a decision as to what exchange rate(s) to use to translate foreign financial statements into the home currency. The objective of this translation process is to measure the *book value* of the company. The choice of exchange rates is complicated by the fact that the transactions reflected in these statements usually have occurred throughout a period during which different exchange rates have prevailed. A decision must be made for each account on whether to use current exchange rates or the exchange rates at the time of the transaction, that is, historical exchange rates.

The U.S. accounting profession's current rule for selecting the exchange rates to be used in the translation process is contained in Statement No. 8 of the Financial Accounting Standards Board. This statement essentially distinguishes between accounts which are measured at cost and at market. Cost figures reflect the historical cost at the time that the transaction was initially recorded. These figures are translated at the exchange rates prevailing at the time of the transaction, that is, at historical exchange rates. Market figures reflect current values. These figures are translated at current exchange rates. Given current accounting practices, FASB #8 specifies the translation practice shown in note 2 to chapter 2. It should be noted that FASB #8 provides a decision rule rather than specific instructions for translation of each account. The decision rule is based on the prices used to measure the account initially— cost or market. If the method of measuring the account is changed, the translation implication will change, without having to alter FASB #8. For example, if inventory were measured in terms of replacement cost, a market price concept, the exchange rate used to translate this account under FASB #8 would be the current exchange rate.

Since some accounts in the balance sheet are translated at historical exchange rates and others at current exchange rates, the balance sheet will rarely balance after this translation process. Only when the amount of assets translated at current exchange rates is the same as the amount of liabilities translated at these rates will the two sides of the balance sheet be in balance. However, in most instances that is not the case, and the difference has to be reconciled in the equity account.

When translated assets exceed the value of translated liabilities, the equity account has to be increased. A foreign-exchange gain takes place. When translated assets are less than translated liabilities, the equity account has to be reduced. A foreign-exchange loss occurs. In the United States the practice of maintaining a clean surplus account mandates that no entry be made directly in the equity account without first being reflected in the income statement. Therefore, the foreign-exchange gains or losses derived from the translation process are shown in the income statement. Foreign-exchange gains and losses affect the period's earnings. If the fluctuations in exchange rates are large, the effects on the income statement and earnings per share can be also very large.

This brief discussion of translation exposure makes it clear how this concept of exposure is closely intertwined with the accountants' rules for the preparation of financial statements. The objective of the translation process is to report the *book value* of different accounts according to accepted accounting principles. In the same manner by which the book value of an account depends on whether it is measured in terms of current prices (market value) or historical prices (cost), the book value of the translated account also depends on whether the exchange rate used for translation is the current exchange rate or the historical exchange rate. The accountants' requirement for consistent reporting practices extends also to the translation process.

Modifications to FASB #8

Before FASB #8 became mandatory in the United States in January 1976, a variety of translation methods were in use. In these other methods inventory was often translated at current exchange rates.[1] If current assets equaled current liabilities, there was no exposure to exchange risk. In addition, foreign-exchange gains and losses derived from this translation process often were not reported in the income statement, but reflected directly in a reserve account in the balance sheet. Needless to say, most criticism of FASB #8 has concentrated on its treatment of inventory and reserves for foreign-exchange gains and losses.[2]

There is nothing which management can do to modify FASB #8 for external reporting purposes, other than to lobby to have it changed. However, management may choose to depart from FASB #8 for internal management purposes. Thus, it is not unusual to hear management defining exposure as "FASB #8 plus inventory." The argument for this departure is that if the liabilities used to finance inventory are translated at current exchange rates, so should the accounts being financed by these liabilities (that is, inventory also should be translated at current exchange rates).

The major accomplishment of this approach is to remove some of the instability in earnings per share produced by the FASB #8 treatment of inventory. When inventory is translated at historical exchange rates, the effect of an exchange rate fluctuation on inventory value is not reflected in the financial statements until the merchandise is sold—usually in the following quarter. In between, the balance sheet tends to appear in a net liability position for translation purposes. In case of an appreciation in the foreign currency the company may have to report a foreign-exchange loss because of the balance sheet position, even though it knows that in the following quarter translated sales will be higher under the new exchange rate. For internal purposes, the translation of inventory at current rates allows management to ignore a translation exposure where the current quarter's effects on exchange gains or losses are compensated for in the following quarter.

This modification to FASB #8 maintains reported *book value* at the core of the exposure definition. However, it departs from the FASB #8 concern for translating accounts at exchange rates corresponding to the period used to price the account. This modified translation measure of exposure effectively uses current exchange rates to translate inventory figures measured at historical cost figures. In exchange for this conceptual inconsistency the modified translation measure accomplishes greater stability in earnings, at least for internal purposes.

The Exchange Traders' Measure: Transaction Exposure

To a trader, the world is made of cash received and cash disbursed. The difference between these two figures is *cash profit*. Exchange risk derives from any fluctuation in exchange rates that can affect the net profit between cash inflows and outflows. If the currency of the cash inflow is different from the currency of the cash outflow, an exchange transaction is necessary before the payment involved in the outflow can be made. The exchange rate prevailing at the time of the exchange transaction is not known until the conversion actually takes place. If the value of the inflow's currency deteriorates relative to the currency needed to realize the payment, the residual profit will decrease and may even become a loss.

Examples of business transactions involving an exchange conversion are the payment in foreign currency for goods purchased by the importer, the receipt of foreign currency in payment for goods sold by the exporter, and the repayment of funds borrowed in foreign currency. The importer and the borrower have to convert their home currency into a foreign currency to realize the payment; the exporter has to convert the foreign currency into the home currency before the funds are made available in the domestic market. In all these cases there are identifiable cash flows which require a transaction in the exchange market. A fluctuation in exchange rates would affect the value of this cash flow and therefore the final *cash profit*—the target of this measure of exposure to exchange risk.

The advantages and disadvantages of both translation and transaction measures of exposure are summarized in table 2A-1.

Table 2A-1
Evaluation of Traditional Exchange Exposure Methods

Advantages	Disadvantages
Translation Exposure	
Consistent from company to company and throughout time.	Inflexible. Does not make allowances for different situations.
Objective. Based on historical records. Does not require subjective evaluation in its computation.	Historical records may be irrelevant to current conditions. Management's analysis of current situation is ignored.
Consistent with traditional computations of book value.	Ignores economic value which may differ greatly from book value.
Transaction Exposure	
Based on future cash flows, the variable relevant to economic value.	Ignores future cash flows which do not involve exchange transaction but which create economic value.
Objective. Concentrates on known future exchange transactions.	Management's evaluation of the impact of exchange fluctuations on operations is ignored.

Notes

1. For a comparison of other translation methods and FASB #8, see Rita M. Rodriguez, "FASB #8: What Has It Done for Us?" *Financial Analysts Journal*, March 1976, pp. 40-48.

2. Another area of criticism of FASB #8 has been its treatment of long-term debt. All debt is translated at current exchange rates under FASB #8, regardless of its maturity. Management often has dealt with this problem by converting foreign currency debt into dollar debt.

3 Financial Markets during 1967–1974

The last section in chapter 2, "Evaluating Alternatives," discussed how exposure risks are compared with hedging costs and how the managers interviewed reached a decision of whether to hedge a fictitious exposure, assuming conditions in the financial markets consistent with efficient markets. In this chapter we question whether the assumption of an efficient market during 1967-1974 is warranted.

Even more than establishing the degree of efficiency in the financial markets, one would want to know how these managers *perceived* the financial markets, regardless of what they actually were. During the interviews managers were asked to develop an "exchange crisis chronology" where they determined whether and when they forecast exchange-rate movements during the relevant period. Unfortunately, most of these managers were reluctant to participate in this exercise, afraid that the benefit of hindsight and the time elapsed would have colored their statements.

In the absence of information on how these managers perceived the financial markets, it became necessary to study the *actual* financial markets and to assume that the perceptions approximated the actual. A thorough analysis of the financial markets is outside the scope of this book. However, an investigation of whether the markets provided any incentive to move funds away from some currencies and into others was essential before the actual flow of funds in these companies could be explained.

Two types of inefficiencies in the market could have influenced these companies to take specific positions in different currencies during 1967-1974. One is the cost of hedging, as measured by the forward rate, relative to the observed changes in the spot rate. If a comparison of these two rates shows a bias throughout the period, then an incentive existed for these companies to move funds in predictable directions. The other type of inefficiency we will examine is the effect of exchange controls imposed by governments. These controls segment the financial markets between domestic and external markets. However, MNCs often have access to both markets. Access to essentially subsidized rates also could have influenced how these companies positioned themselves in different currencies.

The Forward Rate's Forecast

In an efficient market all the information available is incorporated in the observed prices. At the margin, market participants are indifferent to the currency in which they maintain cash balances or denominate their liabilities. Over the long term the returns and costs of the various alternatives should be approximately the same.

For example, at the margin an investor would be indifferent to the choice of holding cash balances in pounds or Swiss francs, even though the interest rate paid on each currency may be different. Because of the presumed efficiency of the market, the currency with depreciation risk will have to pay a higher interest rate to compensate the investor for the risk; the currency with an appreciation risk can pay a lower interest rate and be as desirable as the one with the higher interest rate. In an efficient market the observed rates provide the investor with the same expected yield in both currencies. Any realized exchange gain or loss is expected to be compensated for by the interest rate differential.

An efficient market also provides the investor with indifference as to whether to hold a currency now or purchase it for later delivery. For example, in this market the investor is indifferent between holding pounds or purchasing pounds for delivery three months later in the forward market. The difference in the price of pounds delivered now and pounds delivered three months later is the amount of interest which could be earned on the pound balances during the intervening period compared to what could be earned in another currency, that is, the interest rate differential. This condition is known as interest rate parity.

However, as mentioned above, the interest rate in a currency is affected by its foreign-exchange risk. Depreciating currencies carry higher interest rates than appreciating currencies. Thus the forward rate, which is a function of interest rate differentials, incorporates the market's forecast for the value of a currency. A discount on the forward rate occurs when the market anticipates a depreciation of the currency and this currency carries a higher interest rate. A premium on the forward rate occurs in the case of a currency anticipated to appreciate and carrying a lower interest rate. In this situation there is little incentive, in terms of cash flow gains or losses, to move funds into appreciating currencies and away from depreciating ones. Over the long term the exchange gain which accrues on appreciating currencies is expected to erode by the loss of the higher interest rates which could be earned in depreciating currencies. Similarly, gains in foreign exchange derived from borrowing in depreciating currencies are expected to erode by the high interest rate which has to be paid in these currencies relative to other currencies.

The characteristics of an efficient market just discussed imply that the forward rate is an unbiased forecast of the spot rate. Obviously, these forecasts are subject to error, but over the long run these errors will tend to balance. In any case, in this market it would be impossible to provide forecasts of the spot rate which are consistently superior to the forecasts provided by the forward rate. However, if a consistent bias can be observed in the forward rate's forecasts, inefficiencies in the market can be presumed to exist. Opportunities for profits can be exploited, and the investor is no longer indifferent to holding appreciating or depreciating currencies.

To test whether the forward rate was an unbiased forecaster of the spot rate during 1967-1974, three-month forward rates were compared with the actual spot rates prevailing three months later. The observations corresponded to the middle of February, May, August, and November.[1] Table 3-1 shows the difference between the spot rates anticipated by forward rates and the actual spot rates. In the table the difference is expressed as a *flat* percentage of the actual spot rate; that is, the figures have not been annualized. The differences are summarized in three groups: (1) the cases where the forward-rate forecast overestimated the spot rate by more than 0.5 percent, (2) the cases where the forward-rate forecast the spot rate within 0.5 percent, and (3) the cases where the forward rate underestimated the spot rate by more than 0.5 percent. (Exchange rates in this table are expressed in terms of dollars per unit of foreign currency.)

In every currency, 30 percent or more of the quarters had the spot rate anticipated by the forward rate within 0.5 percent. However, in only three currencies did the forward-rate forecast spot rates that closely in 50 percent or more of the thirty quarters. These currencies are the Canadian dollar, the Belgian franc, and the lira. The forward rate often underestimated or overestimated the spot rate during this period. It certainly was not a very accurate predictor.

Equal uncertainty as to the direction of the forecasting error would be represented by a bell-shaped, or normal, distribution of the forecasting errors. In such a distribution the number of underestimation errors would be approximately the same as the number of overestimation errors. However, table 3-1 shows that there was a tendency for underestimation errors to dominate, that is, a tendency for the forward rate's forecast to be *below* the actual spot rate more often than above it. This is the case in most currencies in the table, with the exception of the guilder and the Swiss franc. For the guilder the percentage of errors is the same on each side. For the Swiss franc the forward rate overestimated the spot rate more often than it underestimated it.

For the six currencies where underestimation errors dominated, this meant that the forward rate tended to underestimate the amount of appreciation and to overestimate the amount of depreciation of these currencies against the dollar, as shown in table 3-2. With interest rate parity holding during the period, the bias in the forward rate means that the interest rates of currencies which both appreciated against the dollar and depreciated against the dollar tended to be higher than justified by future developments in the spot rate. In table 3-2, assuming the dollar interest rate constant, the initial pound interest rate should have been 10 percent instead of 12 percent, and the initial interest rate for the German mark should have been 2 percent instead of 5 percent.

During this period an investor who stayed away from dollars and invested in any of the other currencies made profits more often than losses in foreign exchange. Whenever the forward rate misassessed future spot rates by more

Table 3-1
Spot Rates Compared to Forecast Implied by Earlier Three-Month Forward Rates: 1967-1974, Quarterly
[percentage of total (thirty) observations]

	Canadian Dollar	Pound	Belgian Franc	French Franc	German Mark	Lira	Guilder	Swiss Franc
Three-month forward forecast is more than 0.5% *above* actual spot[a]	17	27	23	23	33	17	30	33
Three-month forward estimated spot within ±0.5% of actual spot[a]	53	37	50	33	30	57	40	43
Three-month forward forecast is more than 0.5% *below* actual spot[a]	30	37	27	43	37	27	30	23
	100	100	100	100	100	100	100	100

Note: Data refer to end of second or third weeks for February, May, August, and November. Exchange rates are measured in terms of U.S. dollars per unit of foreign currency.

[a]Percentages are not annualized. They are a flat percentage of the actual spot rate.

Table 3-2
Characteristic Bias of Forward Rates during 1967-1974

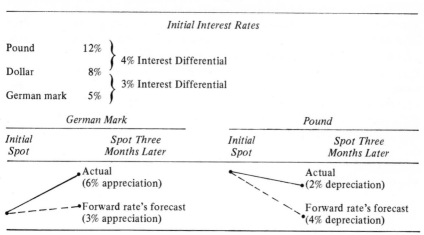

than 0.5 percent, it paid more often than not to borrow dollars and invest in any of the other currencies which either appreciated by more than the loss of interest differentials or depreciated by less than the interest differential in their favor. Similarly, *an investor would have been wise to purchase these other currencies in the forward-exchange market and sell the dollar,* since the actual spot price of these other currencies was often above the rate forecast by the forward rate.[2]

Whether it also paid to borrow currencies depreciating against the dollar in order to invest in currencies appreciating against the dollar depended on the magnitude of the forecast error in the forward rate for each currency. In the example presented above the effective rates, relative to the dollar, after the exchange fluctuations were:

Sterling   12% − 2% depreciation = 10%
Dollar   8%
German mark   5% + 6% appreciation = 11%

Although the cheapest source of funds was the dollar, profits could still be obtained by borrowing sterling and investing in German marks. However, if the appreciation of the mark against the dollar had been only 4 percent, the effective yield of German marks would have been 9 percent, or 5 percent plus 4 percent. In this instance it should have been unprofitable to borrow the currency expected to depreciate against the dollar—sterling—and invest it in the appreciating currency—the German mark.

It could be argued that perhaps the difference between the number of underestimation and overestimation errors was not sufficiently large for most conservative financial officers to want to take exchange positions on this basis. However, when exchange crises finally arrived, many of the positions suggested by the forward rate's underestimation errors would have been amply rewarded. The errors and downward bias of the forward rate's forecast were particularly large when large appreciations or depreciations took place in the exchange markets, as in the last quarter of 1971 and the first half of 1973. (See table 3-3.) If instead of limiting ourselves to the mid-quarter dates, we picked the specific dates when spot rates moved the most (for example, if we picked December 17, 1971, instead of November 12,1971), the profits to be made from borrowing dollars and investing in the other currencies would have been larger than those indicated in table 3-3.

The Impact of Exchange Controls

The literature has presented substantial evidence showing that interest rate parity often holds in the Eurocurrency markets. That is, in these markets interest differentials among currencies in the money market and the premium or discount between the same currencies in the forward-exchange market are approximately the same.[3] However, during the period covered by this book, currencies were often subject to domestic exchange controls. These controls, in fact, segmented the market for the currency between domestic market and Euromarket. The participants in the market were segmented between country residents and everybody else. The country residents had access to the domestic market; everybody else operated only in the Euromarkets. As a result, different prices prevailed in each market. However, MNCs had access to both markets. For example, an MNC with a subsidiary in England could borrow pounds in the domestic market as well as in the Europound market. It could also operate in forward rates prevailing in the Euromarkets.

Foreign-exchange controls on capital outflows from the domestic market, such as the controls in the United Kingdom during the period, produce rates

Table 3-3
Forward Rates: Forecasting Errors during Exchange Crises
(*difference between actual spot rate and forward rate three months earlier,*
as a percentage of the actual spot rate)

Date Spot Observed	Pound	Belgian Franc	French Franc	German Mark	Lira	Guilder	Swiss Franc
November 12, 1971	4		7	4	4	5	
February 9, 1973	6	8	10	9		6	9
May 11, 1973		9	8	16		10	8

in the domestic market which are below the corresponding Eurorates. Conversely, when foreign-exchange controls restrict capital inflows (the Bardepot tax in Germany, for example), domestic rates are higher than the corresponding rates in the Euromarkets. Institutions with access to both markets for a currency, domestic and Euromarkets, can profit from this market segmentation. The higher domestic rates prevailing in the domestic markets of appreciating currencies make it more desirable to hold these currencies. Similarly, access to the lower domestic rates in depreciating currencies makes it more desirable to borrow in those currencies. Access to these domestic markets could enable MNCs to move funds away from depreciating currencies and into appreciating ones at subsidized rates.

One approach to measure the magnitude of the advantage that the universal access to financial markets could confer during 1967-1974 is to measure the incentive to arbitrage between the domestic and the external markets without assuming any risk (that is, on a covered basis). One example of such arbitrage would be the MNC who borrows pounds in the domestic market at a rate lower than for Europounds and then converts the proceeds into dollars and invests them in the Eurodollar market. To protect against the exchange risk involved in borrowing pounds and investing in dollars, the MNC sells the dollars forward against pounds at the higher premium for the dollar prevailing in the Eurocurrency markets than in the domestic market. If the borrowings had been made in the Euromarkets, interest parity would have prevented any substantial profit in this transaction. However, since the MNC had access to the domestic pound market, it could borrow at a lower rate in that market and profit from moving funds from that currency into dollars. The actual mechanics of this transaction would have the local subsidiary borrow domestic pounds and transfer them to the parent company (for example, as a prepayment of a payable to the parent). The parent company would then invest the proceeds in Eurodollars and simultaneously sell dollars forward against sterling in the external market.

It must be noted that in the arbitrage transaction just discussed (a swap), the MNC did not alter its exchange position, although it could profit from the transaction.[4] The "buy" of dollars and the "sell" of pounds in the money market are compensated by the "sell" of dollars and the "buy" of pounds in the forward market. There is no exchange risk in the transaction, and therefore it cannot be used to eliminate or create an exchange position. However, to the extent that opportunities for this kind of arbitrage existed during 1967-1974, the MNCs could have modified their exchange positions at rates subsidized by the exchange controls. For example, a company wishing to have a negative exposure in pounds and a positive one in guilders could do so by borrowing pounds at the lower domestic rate, instead of Europounds, and investing the proceeds in guilders. For the transaction to be profitable, the depreciation of the pound against the guilder could be smaller than if pounds had been borrowed in the Europound market.

Even if in the external market the forward rate had been an unbiased predictor of the spot rate, as discussed in an earlier section, access to the domestic pound market provided the MNCs with biased rates. The domestic pound rates, relative to the external ones, underestimated the expected depreciation of the pound. In other words, access to the domestic pound market reduced the cost of holding the short position in pounds. Exchange controls effectively subsidized speculation for those with access to both domestic and external markets.

Table 3-4 summarizes the number of cases during 1967-1974 in which an incentive for covered interest arbitrage of the kind just described was found. These computations use three-month Eurodollar deposit rates and domestic prime lending rates as the rates available for investing and borrowing. The rate used for covering the transaction is the forward rate prevailing in the external market.

In all currencies, with the exception of the Canadian dollar, the majority of quarters provided an incentive to arbitrage funds between the domestic and the external markets. Even for the Canadian dollar, where in 42 percent of the quarters there was not much incentive for arbitrage in either direction, an almost equal number of quarters, 39 percent, provided incentive for borrowing Canadian dollars on a covered basis. Table 3-4 shows that for the Canadian dollar, the pound, and the lira the MNC could have profited by more than 0.5 percent per annum in 39 percent or more of the quarters by doing the following: borrowing the local currency at the prime rate in the domestic market and investing the proceeds in Eurodollar deposits on a covered basis (that is, sell dollars against the foreign currency in the forward market). In these cases the loss in interest rate between high domestic borrowing rates and low Eurodollar rates is more than compensated for by the premium that the MNC can realize in selling the dollar against the local currency in the forward market (based on Eurorates) to cover the transaction. That is, borrowing in these currencies without undertaking any foreign-exchange risk would have provided profits for the MNCs in a large number of quarters during 1967-1974.

The interest arbitrage incentive works in the opposite direction in the majority of observations for the Belgian and French francs, the German mark, the lira, the guilder, and the Swiss franc. (Notice that the lira is listed with both groups of currencies: the ones with a large number of quarters with an incentive to borrow the local currency and the ones with a large number of quarters with an incentive to invest in the local currency.) In these cases, the interest arbitrage indicates that profits could have been made by borrowing funds at relatively high interest rates in the Eurodollar market and investing them on a covered basis in the respective domestic markets at a lower interest rate. The loss in interest would have been more than compensated for by the premium in the forward market which these currencies demanded.

It can be argued that some of these incentives to borrow dollars and invest in the domestic market would disappear if (1) the MNC could invest not at the prime rate but only at a lower rate such as Treasury bills and if (2) the MNC

Table 3-4
Interest Arbitrage Incentive between Domestic Foreign Currency Markets and the Eurodollar Market: 1967-1974, Quarterly
[percentage of total (thirty-one) observations]

	Canadian Dollar	Pound	Belgian Franc	French Franc	German Mark	Lira	Guilder	Swiss Franc
Profit by more than 0.5% per annum by *borrowing foreign currency* in domestic market and investing in Eurodollars on a covered basis[a]	39	68	29	29	0	42	9	26
Interest arbitrage incentive within ± 0.5% per annum	42	16	13	3	6	10	26	16
Profit by more than 0.5% per annum by *investing in foreign currency* with borrowed Eurodollars on a covered basis[b]	19	16	58	68	94	48	65	58
	100	100	100	100	100	100	100	100

Note: Data refer to end of second or third weeks for February, May, August, and November.

[a]The cover consists of selling dollars in the forward market against the borrowed currency.

[b]The cover consists of selling the currency invested in the forward market against dollars.

had to borrow at a substantial rate above the Eurodollar deposit rate. Indeed, when the Treasury bill rate was substituted for the prime rate, many of the incentives to invest in the domestic market disappeared. Still, during crises many of these incentives remained. (See table 3-5.)

In any case, the relevant test would be the size of the spread between the prime lending rate and the deposit rate available to the MNC in the domestic market. If this spread was smaller than the percentage calculated for the incentive to invest at the prime rate, the MNCs still had an incentive to invest in the domestic market on a covered basis. For the mark and the Swiss franc in particular, the incentive to invest calculated using the prime rate was above 3 percent on most dates. If the spread between the prime rate and the deposit rate available to the MNC in the domestic market was less than 3 percent, which is very likely to have been the case, the MNC would still have benefited from borrowing Eurodollars and investing the proceeds in German marks or Swiss francs in the domestic market on a covered basis.

Foreign-exchange controls during 1967-1974 produced domestic interest rates on the pound and the lira lower than the corresponding Eurorates, on which the forward rate is based. Also, the domestic rates in Belgium, France, Germany, the Netherlands, and Switzerland were higher than their counterparts in the Eurocurrency markets. Thus, the data in table 3-4 support the contention that *market imperfections often made it economical for MNCs to borrow in the traditionally weak currencies, pounds and lire, and accumulate resources in the traditionally appreciating currencies, German marks, guilders, Swiss francs, and so on.*

Summary

Data presented in this chapter suggest that the exchange forecasts implied by forward rates during 1967-1974 were biased in a manner which often made it profitable to stay away from dollars, and possibly other depreciating currencies,

Table 3-5
Interest Arbitrage Incentive during Exchange Crises
(percentage per annum profit from borrowing Eurodollars and investing in domestic Treasury bills on a covered basis)

Date	Belgian Franc	French Franc	German Mark	Guilder
February 12, 1971	1		1	1.5
August 13, 1971	1	3		
February 9, 1973	1		4	0.5
May 11, 1973			3	

and invest in appreciating currencies. Exchange controls imposed by various governments tended to subsidize this operation. Even managers who did not want to speculate in the exchange markets on the basis of these inefficiencies would have found it difficult to ignore them in managing their companies' exposure to exchange risk.

In the next two chapters currencies are characterized as "strong" or "weak." This is done on the most clear-cut basis presented in this chapter: the market segmentation produced by exchange controls. Strong currencies are identified as those where the majority of quarters provided an incentive for investing in those currencies on a covered basis. These are the Belgian franc, the French franc, the German mark, the guilder, and the Swiss franc. To this list the yen will be added. This currency could not be examined in this chapter since a significant external yen market did not exist during the period of study. However, the appreciating nature of that currency and the strong government controls in that country warrant including the yen with the other strong currencies.

It will be noted that the lira was excluded from the group of strong currencies. Although the majority of quarters, 48 percent, provided an incentive for investing in lire, a very large number of quarters, 42 percent, had an incentive for borrowing lire. So, the lira was included in the group of weak currencies. The other two currencies labeled as weak are the pound and the Canadian dollar. In a majority of quarters observed, 68 percent, there was an incentive to borrow in pounds. However, the Canadian dollar actually had a majority of the quarters, 42 percent, characterized as providing no incentive. But the fact that in 39 percent of the quarters the incentive was to borrow (in contrast to 19 percent to invest) made it desirable to classify the Canadian dollar with the weak currencies.

In summary, we have the following grouping of currencies:

Appreciating or Strong	*Depreciating or Weak*
Belgian franc	Canadian dollar
French franc	Lira
German mark	Pound
Guilder	
Swiss franc	
Yen	

In all appreciating or strong currencies, the incentive was clearly to invest. However, among the depreciating or weak currencies, only the pound had a dominant number of quarters making it profitable to borrow domestic pounds. For the period as a whole, labeling the Canadian dollar and the lira as weak currencies is somewhat arguable. The main contribution of this classification is to separate the stronger currencies from the other currencies, although among the other currencies the weak nature of the pound was common throughout the period.

Notes

1. Mid-quarter and mid-month data were chosen to avoid the irregularities introduced by window-dressing transactions at the end of the month. It will be noted also that the observations do not overlap. This avoids another potential source of bias.

2. This contrasts with the results of Giddy and Dufey who conclude that the foreign-exchange market is an efficient market. See Ian H. Giddy and Gunter Dufey, "The Random Behavior of Flexible Exchange Rates: Implications for Forecasting," *Journal of International Business Studies*, Spring 1975, pp. 1-32.

3. See Jacob A. Frenkel and Richard M. Levich, "Transaction Costs and Interest Arbitrage: Tranquil versus Turbulent Periods," *Journal of Political Economy*, December 1977, pp. 1209-1226.

4. For a detailed explanation of swap transactions see Heinz Riehl and Rita M. Rodriguez, *Foreign Exchange Markets* (New York: McGraw-Hill, 1977).

4

Exchange-Management Decisions during 1967-1974

In this chapter and the following one the line of inquiry into the behavior of MNCs is reversed. In chapter 2 we asked managers how they reached foreign-exchange management decisions. Now we ask the questions from the historical figures reflecting those decisions. We ask: What were the managers doing with exposure to exchange risk? We ignore most of the information presented in chapter 2 and begin by hypothesizing a range of possible managerial behaviors which can then be tested against the historical figures.[1]

A Taxonomy of Managerial Behavior

This taxonomy is defined in terms of both the managers' attitudes toward exchange risk and the nature of the financial markets. The attitudes toward risk are divided into three major groups: risk-paranoid, risk-neutral, and risk-asymmetrical. Financial markets are assumed to be either efficient or inefficient.

The managers in each risk group can be expected to follow a different policy toward the management of exchange risk, depending on the kind of financial market they face. Let's examine the policy implications of the various combinations of risk attitude and market characteristic.

Risk-Paranoid

In this group any exposure to exchange risk is intolerable. The primary objective of exposure management becomes to reduce the exposure to zero, regardless of the costs involved.

1. If there are inefficiencies in the markets, this policy will deprive the company of potential savings in interest costs or of gains in foreign exchange (depending on which inefficiencies exist). However, the firm may feel that the cost of finding the necessary information, given its position in the market, is not worth the potential savings or gains.

2. If markets are perceived to be efficient, management chooses to save itself the nuisance of showing temporary exchange gains and losses, even though they would neutralize each other over the long term, and tries to maintain zero exposure in each currency. The company would expect the cost of this policy to be mainly transactions costs.

Risk-Neutral

All risk involves some returns and possible costs. To management in this group the risk acceptable in an exchange exposure is a function of the tradeoffs between possible returns and costs involved in maintaining the exposure versus eliminating it. In this tradeoff a dollar of possible loss due to exposure is comparable to a dollar of cost involved in reducing the exposure. The specific policy which management will follow depends on the nature of the inefficiencies in the market.

1. If the forecast implied by interest rate differentials and the forward rate is felt to *underestimate* the future *level* of spot exchange rates (for example, a currency is expected to devalue by a percentage larger than the one implied by the higher interest rate it commands over the other currencies), the company will borrow funds in the relatively high-interest currency, the weak currency, and invest in the relatively low-interest currency, the strong currency (that is, be short in depreciating currencies and long in appreciating currencies). The loss in interest is expected to be more than compensated for by the gains in foreign exchange.

2. If the forecast implied by interest rate differentials and the forward rate is felt to *overestimate* the future *level* of spot rates (for example, a currency is expected to devalue by a percentage smaller than the one implied by the higher interest rate it commands over other currencies), management will borrow funds in low-interest currencies, strong currencies, and invest in high-interest currencies, weak currencies (that is, be long in depreciating currencies and short in appreciating currencies). The profit derived from interest differentials is expected to more than compensate for the exchange loss.

3. If markets are considered to be efficient, management will ignore foreign-exchange risks and interest data and will operate on the basis of long-term business considerations (say, maintain a presence in different financial markets). The observed exposures under these circumstances will tend to be random, dictated by whatever financial arrangement may help promote the basic nature of the business.

Risk-Asymmetrical

Partially because of reporting considerations, management in this category considers one dollar of exchange loss more expensive than one dollar of interest cost. If the exposure involves likely exchange losses, management will tend to close the position, even if the costs of closing the position exceed the expected exchange losses. However, if the most likely outcome of the exposure is an exchange gain, management is often willing to live with this risk, as long as the costs of maintaining the position do not exceed the expected exchange gains. The objective of this group is also to minimize exchange risk; however, more weight is placed on reporting one dollar of exchange losses than on reporting one dollar of exchange gains, given the same costs to close the position.

1. If markets are perceived to be inefficient, financial policies which indicate an expected gain in foreign exchange will be followed to the extent that possible losses, in a statistical sense, do not exceed a certain amount. Alternatively, financial policies which indicate an expected exchange loss, justified because of the benefits derived from interest differentials, will not be followed unless the impact of the exchange loss is tolerable to management. With inefficient markets, this attitude introduces a bias toward a positive exposure in appreciating currencies and a negative exposure in depreciating ones.

2. If markets are expected to be efficient, the transaction costs incurred over the long term to reduce all exposures to zero are considered worth the elimination of exchange losses.

A summary of the net exposures expected under various combinations of management's attitudes toward exchange risk and expected market behavior is presented in table 4-1.

The tabulation in table 4-1 can be simplified by concentrating on the market inefficiencies which we found to be most prevalent in chapter 3. Those inefficiencies often favored borrowing depreciating currencies and investing in appreciating currencies. We can concentrate on this type of inefficiency even if we assume the external markets to be efficient, but acknowledge the

Table 4-1
Expected Net Exposures under Various Combinations of Management's Risk Attitudes and Perceptions of Markets

| | | Management's Perception of Markets | |
| | | Market Inefficiencies Suggesting a Position which Is: | |
Management's Risk Attitude	Efficient Markets	Long in High-Interest (Depreciating) Currencies; Short in Low-Interest (Appreciating) Currencies	Long in Low-Interest (Appreciating) Currencies; Short in High-Interest (Depreciating) Currencies
Risk-paranoid	0	0	0
Risk-neutral	Random	Long in high-interest (depreciating) currencies; short in low-interest (appreciating) currencies	Long in low-interest (appreciating) currencies; short in high-interest (depreciating) currencies
Risk-asymmetrical	0	As above, subject to maximum exchange loss constraint	As above, subject to maximum exchange loss constraint

existence of government exchange controls during the period. As discussed in chapter 3, these controls usually restrict outflows from depreciating currencies and inflows into appreciating currencies. As a result, the interest rates for weaker currencies are lower in the domestic market than in the external market. The opposite is true for stronger currencies. If we assume the rates in the external markets incorporate all market's expectations, the MNC with access to domestic markets will want to borrow in the domestic market of the weaker currency and invest the proceeds in the domestic market of the stronger currency, that is, be short in the depreciating currency and long in the appreciating one.

The possible perceptions of the exchange markets in table 4-1 have been reduced to two: efficient markets and markets which favor investing in appreciating currencies and borrowing in depreciating ones. The rest of this chapter tries to establish which one of the remaining six possible combinations of risk attitude and market perception is best supported by the empirical data.

Empirical Evidence

The Data

Gathering exposure figures from the participating companies meant gathering exposure figures as calculated for translation purposes. To the extent that exposure reports were maintained, these referred mostly to the accounts exposed in the balance sheet. For the companies which did not have an exposure reporting system during this period, financial statements were the only available source of historical exposure. In addition, balance sheet exposure is the exposure which these companies thought to be the most important exposure during the period of interest.[2]

Data on exposure to exchange risk were collected from thirty-six of the seventy companies interviewed. (The list of participating companies shown in appendix A indicates which companies contributed quantitative data.) The data represent the major European and Japanese subsidiaries for each of the companies. Finance subsidiaries, when present, also were included in the sample. For each of these subsidiaries, data were compiled for all or a majority of the balance sheet accounts on a currency-by-currency basis at quarterly intervals. The amounts of forward-exchange contracts outstanding on the date of the balance sheets also were gathered.

In fifteen of the participating companies the figures were disaggregated by currency in the form of so-called exposure reports. In the other companies, the disaggregation of balance sheets by currency was derived from tables used by the company in the process of consolidating its financial statements. The period intended to be covered was 1967 to mid-1974 by quarters. However, less than one-third of the companies were able to furnish data for the earlier years. All data are expressed in terms of 1968 exchange rates.

Testing for the Presence of Extremes

In searching for the cell which is best supported by the data it is easiest to test first those which represent extremes. These are the cells involving the risk attitude labeled "risk-paranoid" and the perception of a market which is totally efficient, that is, the first row and the first column to the left in table 4-1.

The Risk-Paranoid Syndrome. Firms that find any foreign-exchange risk intolerable, whether they believe the markets to be efficient or not, will always try to reduce exposure to zero. This attitude leads one to expect the average net exposure adjusted by outstanding forward contracts in each currency to be close to zero. Companies following this policy would be expected to have hedged whatever exposure they might otherwise have recorded. Thus, by observing how often companies maintained a zero adjusted exposure on average, one can estimate the prevalence of the position of a strong risk aversion.

For each company the *arithmetic* mean of the exposure for all the quarters in each currency was computed. Table 4-2 shows for each currency the number of companies where the mean exposure for the whole period can be considered to be zero and the number of instances where a nonzero mean is supported by statistical tests.[3] *A large majority of companies reported average levels of exposure in each currency which were statistically different from zero.* All currencies show that 59 percent or more of the companies reporting in that currency had average levels of exposure significantly different from zero.

Table 4-2 aggregates companies on a currency basis. In this approach the behavior of specific companies across currencies is obscured. To analyze the extent to which companies' policies differed, the number of currencies with average levels significantly different from zero was calculated separately for each company. The results of this approach showed that twenty-six companies had more than 75 percent of the reporting currencies with nonzero average levels; thirty-three companies (including the twenty-six firms with more than 75 percent) had more than 50 percent of nonzero average levels.

The evidence presented in table 4-2 and the facts for specific companies indicate a strong inclination for companies to have exposures which, on average, are different from zero after the outstanding foreign-exchange contracts are taken into account. At best, one can say that three out of thirty-six companies may be pursuing a policy of zero exposure in the aggregate. *A management policy of always reducing exchange risk to zero does not appear to prevail. Foreign-exchange risk paranoia does not appear to dominate management's policies.*

The Belief that Markets Are Efficient. If managers perceived financial markets to be efficient, the previous findings are consistent with only one possible risk attitude: what has been labeled "risk-neutral." The combination of efficient markets and risk-asymmetrical attitudes can be eliminated since it suggested

Table 4-2
Average Exposure Levels: Companies Reporting Zero and Nonzero Levels
(*95 percent confidence level, deflated data*)

	Reporting Currency									
	U.S. Dollar	French Franc	German Mark	Lira	Pound	Swiss Franc	Guilder	Belgian Franc	Yen	Canadian Dollar
Number of companies reporting currency	28	30	31	27	33	22	25	18	14	13
Number of companies reporting exposure levels significantly different from zero	25	24	25	17	23	13	21	12	12	13
Percentage of companies with exposure levels significantly different from zero	89	80	81	63	70	59	84	67	86	100
Percentage of companies with exposure levels equal to zero or insignificantly different from zero	11	20	19	37	30	41	16	33	14	0

Note: Exposure is defined as company's exposure definition for accounting purposes plus outstanding forward exchange contracts.

zero exposure. The data just examined are not consistent with any policy which sought to reduce exposures to zero. That is how the risk-paranoid attitude, regardless of the perceived market, also was eliminated.

The risk-neutral manager operating in what is perceived to be an efficient market expects foreign-exchange gains and losses to neutralize one another over the long term. In this environment a policy of reducing exposure to zero would produce only transaction costs. So, the manager operating purely on the basis of total gains and losses would expect zero gains or losses if foreign-exchange risk is ignored and a loss if the risk is covered constantly. The no-cover policy dominates.

A no-cover policy would show, for the most part, average *levels* of exposure different from zero. The nature of business operations would dictate the actual level. However, the *changes* in exposure would not be very different from zero. Business operating conditions, with the exception of seasonal fluctuations, would not produce very large changes in exposure from quarter to quarter. Thus, to test whether these managers acted as if the markets were efficient, we can test whether the *changes* in exposure were significantly different from zero.

Changes in exposure were measured in terms of percentages computed according to the simple formula

$$\text{Percentage change} = \frac{t_1 - t_0}{t_0}$$

The use of percentages has the advantage of placing all the currencies on the same scale. For purposes of computing aggregate changes, *absolute* changes were used.[4] The percentage changes were computed with the exposure in each currency expressed in various ways, as discussed below.

The simplest measure of change is quarter-to-quarter absolute changes. In table 4-3 this measure shows that in seven major currencies more than 50 percent of companies reported significant changes in exposure. The currencies where less than 50 percent of companies reported significant changes are the Swiss franc, the guilder, and the yen. A vast majority of companies in most currencies had large changes in their exposures. *The policy of ignoring the foreign-exchange market (presumably because it is assumed to be efficient) is not supported by these data.*

The other measure of change in table 4-3 is quarter-to-quarter changes in the percentage of total exposure represented by each currency. This measure refines the earlier measure of change by placing exposure within the perspective of total exposure for the company. This measure allows one to approach the issue of whether management views all the currency components of the total exposure as a whole vis-à-vis the U.S. dollar or whether each currency situation relative to the U.S. dollar is handled separately. If management's policies were based on certain conceptions as to the situation of all currencies relative to the U.S. dollar, one would not observe significant changes in the percentage of total exposure represented by each currency. For example, if management's belief were that all currencies would strengthen against the U.S. dollar, one might expect an increase in the company's total exposure to foreign-exchange risk. However, the percentage of that exposure represented by each currency should remain fairly stable. If, on the other hand, management thought of currencies in isolation or in subgroups, then one would expect the exposure represented by each currency to fluctuate by a percentage different from the variation in total exposure.

Table 4-3 shows that *the percentage of foreign-exchange exposure represented by each currency changes significantly on numerous occasions. Management's attitude toward foreign-exchange risk in each currency appears to be either selective or random, not uniform* (or exposure in each currency is determined by a set of variables which is different for each currency). A view of "all currencies against the U.S. dollar" as the basis for decision making on exposure is not supported.[5]

Testing for Behavior Consistent with
Market Imperfections

Earlier we restricted the types of possible market imperfection to those which are most typical—those produced by government exchange controls. This eliminated the column to the right in table 4-1. In the preceding section we dismissed the presence of extreme policies in exchange management, such as always reducing exposure to zero or disregarding the fluctuations in exchange rates because markets are efficient. This eliminated the top row and the column to the left in table 4-1. So we are left with only the lower two cells in the center column of table 4-1. Apparently, managers saw some degree of imperfection in the financial markets, and they were either neutral or particularly averse to bearing foreign-exchange risk, but they were not paranoid in refusing to accept any risk.

Table 4-1 suggests the positions which MNCs with access to domestic markets would want to assume to take advantage of the market imperfections created by exchange controls. To test whether managers followed the incentives created by this situation, one has to distinguish what currencies were depreciating and subject to capital outflow controls and which ones were appreciating and subject to capital inflow controls.

The currencies were divided into two groups: currencies which tended to appreciate throughout 1967-1974 and those which tended to decline or remain constant against the U.S. dollar during that time. This classification was done on the basis of the nature of the exchange controls prevailing throughout the period, as discussed in chapter 3. Thus, the currencies of interest were classified as follows:

Table 4-3
Average Quarterly Changes in Exposure: Companies Reporting Changes Significantly Different from Zero
(*95 percent confidence level, deflated data*)

	U.S. Dollar	French Franc	German Mark	Lira	Pound	Swiss Franc	Guilder	Belgian Franc	Yen	Canadian Dollar
Number of companies reporting currency	27	29	31	26	33	20	23	18	13	12
Number of companies reporting changes significantly different from zero										
Absolute changes	14	19	16	18	18	8	9	10	6	7
Changes in percentage of exposure	21	26	25	22	29	15	18	14	11	9
Percentage of companies with significant changes										
Absolute changes	52	66	52	69	54	40	39	56	46	58
Changes in percentage of exposure	78	90	81	85	88	75	78	78	84	75

Note: Exposure is defined as company's exposure definition for accounting purposes plus outstanding forward exchange contracts.

Appreciating or Strong	*Depreciating or Weak*
French franc	U.S. dollar
German mark	Lira
Swiss franc	Pound
Guilder	Canadian dollar
Belgian franc	
Yen	

To the extent that the market imperfections triggered by the segmentation between domestic and Eurocurrency markets were an important determinant of the behavior of the accounts studied, we should expect the following types of net exposures and changes in the component accounts:

Appreciating currencies:
Net exposure: net asset position
Assets: positive changes larger than negative changes
Liabilities: negative changes larger than positive changes

Depreciating currencies:
Net exposure: net liability position
Assets: negative changes larger than positive changes
Liabilities: positive changes larger than negative changes

Net Exposure. Table 4-4 shows the sign of average levels of exposures and the nature of the quarterly changes in those exposures for the currencies reported by the companies in the sample. The average of changes is now computed separately for positive changes and negative changes.[6]

The average level of exposure is more often positive than negative in most currencies. These currencies include the U.S. dollar, the French franc, the German mark, the pound, the guilder, the Belgian franc, and the Canadian dollar. In yen, an equal number of companies reported positive average exposures and negative ones. In lira, a slightly higher number of companies reported negative average exposures. The vast majority of the companies in the sample reported a negative exposure in Swiss francs.

To the extent that market inefficiencies produced by exchange controls exercised a strong influence in the determination of these companies' net exposure, the most puzzling outcomes shown in table 4-4 are the large number of companies reporting average positive exposures in pounds and the large number reporting negative exposures in Swiss francs. The incentives to profit from exchange controls on these currencies would have predicted a prevalence of signs for the exposure in these currencies exactly *opposite* to the ones observed.

The analysis of average quarterly *changes* sheds additional light on the findings regarding the average *levels* of exposure. With the exception of the yen, in every currency most companies have the average of positive changes

Table 4-4
Net Exposure: Average Levels and Average Quarterly Changes

	U.S. Dollar	French Franc	German Mark	Lira	Pound	Swiss Franc	Guilder	Belgian Franc	Yen	Canadian Dollar	Total
Number of companies with significant[a] average positive exposure	20	17	19	12	19	4	16	10	6	10	133
Number of companies with significant average negative exposure	7	10	11	14	14	14	7	7	6	1	91
Total	27	27	30	26	33	18	23	17	12	11	224
Number of companies with positive changes greater than negative changes	15	16	21	14	22	10	16	11	5	8	138
Number of companies with negative changes greater than positive changes	12	11	9	12	11	8	7	6	7	3	86
Total	27	27	30	26	33	18	23	17	12	11	224

Note: Net exposure is defined as company's exposure definition plus outstanding forward exchange contracts.

[a]Statistical significance has been found by testing the null hypothesis that mean level is zero. The "Student's *t*" distribution was used to conduct the test.

larger than the average of negative changes. Although not shown in this table, usually there are a larger *number* of positive changes than negative changes. Therefore, on average, the absolute amount of change was larger in the case of positive changes than in the case of negative changes. This provides some explanation for the prevalence of positive over negative exposures, including the pound and the U.S. dollar. In the case of the Swiss franc, one must assume a very large negative exposure at the beginning of the period which does not turn into a positive exposure in spite of the recurrent positive changes in this currency.

What forces were behind this tendency to produce positive changes and positive levels in net exposure?

The Accounts behind Net Exposure. I have analyzed seven specific accounts: cash and marketable securities, accounts receivable, inventory, accounts payable, short-term debt, long-term debt, and forward-foreign-exchange contracts.[7] Of these accounts, inventory and long-term debt were not always included in the definition of exposure used by each company. The major concern of management was the specific accounts included in the definition of exposure. However, attention was also paid to the other accounts which could be subject to exposure to foreign-exchange risk in purely economic terms or manipulated to alter exposure as defined by the accountants.

Table 4-5 shows, for each of the accounts mentioned, the number of companies in each currency where the average positive change was larger than the average negative change and the number of companies where the opposite relationship prevailed. The message of this table is clear throughout all entries: Most companies, in all their accounts, and in almost every single currency, had the average positive changes larger than the average negative changes. The exceptions were very few and occur in forward contracts and long-term debt. Negative changes were larger than positive changes in the case of forward contracts in pounds, and in the cases of long-term debt in lira, guilders, and Belgian francs.

Although the unit of measurement is quarter-to-quarter change, an underlying growth trend appears to dominate the picture to produce larger positive changes than negative changes. We know that international business was growing and that U.S. companies were expanding abroad extensively during the period covered. However, is it possible that this single fact could account for the performance of net exposure as well as the component accounts? Interviews with management revealed a very deep concern with the issue of exposure to foreign-exchange risk. Given this concern, the discretionary financial power that a multinational company is capable of wielding, and the arbitrage incentives available to MNCs, it is hard to believe that growth alone accounted for these findings.[8]

The effects of growth on exposure to exchange risk are most direct on the accounts reflecting marketing and production decisions. A firm operating a retail business in Italy would have little choice but to have its receivables denominated in lire. However, the financing of these receivables need not be

Table 4-5
Individual Accounts: Comparison of Average Positive and Average Negative Changes in Each Company

	U.S. Dollar	French Franc	German Mark	Lira	Pound	Swiss Franc	Guilder	Belgian Franc	Yen	Canadian Dollar	Total
					Number of Companies						
Cash											
↑ > ↓	8	17	16	13	17	12	13	7	6	5	114
↑ < ↓	3	4	5	2	5	2	1	1	3	1	27
Total	11	21	21	15	22	14	14	8	9	6	141
Forward contracts											
↑ > ↓	10	5	5	3	3	1	0	3	3	—	33
↑ < ↓	7	2	2	1	11	2	2	0	0	—	27
Total	17	7	7	4	14	3	2	3	3	—	60
Accounts receivable											
↑ > ↓	6	19	19	17	20	8	16	7	10	7	129
↑ < ↓	5	5	4	1	5	4	5	5	0	0	34
Total	11	24	23	18	25	12	21	12	10	7	163
Inventory											
↑ > ↓	3	17	13	12	19	3	9	8	4	4	92
↑ < ↓	2	2	4	5	2	1	2	1	2	2	23
Total	5	19	17	17	21	4	11	9	6	6	115
Accounts payable											
↑ > ↓	6	12	10	14	15	5	8	8	7	1	86
↑ < ↓	2	4	6	1	2	2	7	1	0	2	27
Total	8	16	16	15	17	7	15	9	7	3	113
Short-term debt											
↑ > ↓	4	17	15	14	17	5	7	8	5	4	96
↑ < ↓	6	3	4	2	5	5	3	2	2	3	35
Total	10	20	19	16	22	10	10	10	7	7	131
Long-term debt											
↑ > ↓	3	8	6	1	6	3	0	0	2	1	30
↑ < ↓	1	5	4	8	5	2	3	2	1	1	32
Total	4	13	10	9	11	5	3	2	3	2	62

↑ = average positive percentage change; ↓ = average negative percentage change.

in lire; it could be in any currency, as long as the manager was willing to accept the exposure implications.

To incorporate the difference in flexibility to denominate the currency of an account, the accounts in the study were divided between those which the financial manager was endowed with from operations and those where he or she had flexibility to pursue by the desired exposure policy. The two groups of accounts have been labeled *operating accounts* and *financing accounts*. In the operating accounts, the assumption is that considerations more akin to the intrinsic nature of the business (say, marketing strategy) dominate the decision about the currency of denomination. These accounts are accounts receivable, inventory, and accounts payable. The financing accounts are considered to be the ones where the financial officer has the most discretionary power as to the currency of denomination. These accounts are cash, forward-exchange contracts, short-term debt, and long-term debt.

Before aggregating the accounts into the two groups for each company, the average change in each account was computed. This was done by multiplying the average quarterly change in each account by the average size of the account for the period. These average changes were then aggregated, so for each company the aggregate changes in financing and operating accounts represent the sum of the changes in the component accounts weighed by the size of the account.

Table 4-6 shows the percentage of companies reporting either positive or negative average changes in the operating and the financing accounts. As anticipated, the growth in international business of these companies tended to produce positive exposures in the operating accounts. In every currency, more than half of the companies had their operating accounts generating positive exposures on average. For financing accounts, however, the picture was not so homogeneous.

As described earlier in this section, the market inefficiencies postulated in this chapter would have the financial officer who took advantage of them trying to make the exposures less negative or more positive in the appreciating currencies. In our classification these are the French franc, the German mark, the Swiss franc, the guilder, the Belgian franc, and the yen. In depreciating currencies, the officer would be trying to make the exposures more negative or less positive. In our classification the depreciating currencies are the lira, the pound, and the Canadian dollar.

Table 4-6 shows that more than half of the companies reporting in the given currency took advantage of the presumed inefficiency in the capital markets in the following currencies:

Percentage of Companies with Financial
Flows in Direction:

	As Expected	*Contrary to Expected*
Lira	55	49
Pound	65	37
Swiss franc	70	30
Guilder	81	19
Belgian franc	62	38

Table 4-6

Characteristic Behavior and Relationship between Changes in Operating and Financing Accounts

(percentage of companies reporting in the given currency)

	U.S. Dollar	French Franc	German Mark	Lira	Pound	Swiss Franc	Guilder	Belgian Franc	Yen	Canadian Dollar
Operating accounts tended to generate:										
Positive exposures	54	80	65	65	75	54	87	61	90	91
Negative exposures	47	20	34	40	27	46	13	39	9	13
	100	100	100	100	100	100	100	100	100	100
Financing accounts tended to generate:										
Positive exposures	62	50	42	49	37	70	81	62	45	52
Negative exposures	39	50	57	55	65	30	19	38	54	52
	100	100	100	100	100	100	100	100	100	100
Financing accounts *reinforced* tendency of operating accounts to generate positive exposures	31	38	30	34	29	39	68	31	36	39
Financing accounts *counteracted* tendency of operating accounts to generate positive exposures	23	42	35	30	46	15	19	30	54	52
Financing accounts *reinforced* tendency of operating accounts to generate negative exposures	16	8	22	25	19	15	–	8	–	–
Financing accounts *counteracted* tendency of operating accounts to generate negative exposures	31	12	12	15	8	31	13	31	9	13
	100	100	100	100	100	100	100	100	100	100

Note: Percentages do not always add to 100 because of rounding error.

In the following currencies most of the companies reporting in them had their financial flows move in the direction opposite from the one expected from market imperfections:

	Percentage of Companies with Financial Flows in Direction:	
	As Expected	*Contrary to Expected*
German mark	42	57
Yen	45	54

Finally, as many companies moved their financial accounts in the direction expected as in the opposite direction in the following currencies: French franc and Canadian dollar.

In most of the currencies the majority of the companies moved their financial flows in a manner consistent with taking advantage of the postulated market imperfections. The major exceptions are the German mark and the yen. Greater difficulty in having access to the domestic capital markets of these currencies than to the domestic markets of the other currencies may account for these findings. Most observers would agree that the Japanese and the German authorities have been particularly strict in enforcing the spirit of their foreign-exchange controls.

What Risk Attitude?

Now that we have found a degree of support for the perception of markets which are inefficient, we must search for what risk attitude is most consistent with the data. Since we eliminated the risk-paranoid attitude earlier, we must now choose between the attitudes labeled "risk-neutral" and "risk-asymmetrical."

Assuming the financial officer had complete freedom to determine net exposures in each currency, subject to the constraints imposed by the market, we could interpret the observed net exposures in the following manner:

1. Right exposures (long in appreciating currencies and short in depreciating ones) would be caused by risk-*neutral* or risk-*asymmetrical* MNCs taking advantage of the disequilibrium between domestic and Euromarkets; or if access to domestic financial markets was limited, a risk aversion which was *asymmetrical*; greater against exchange losses than against exchange gains.
2. Wrong exposures (short in appreciating currencies and long in depreciating ones) would be caused by lack of sufficient access to domestic financial markets in an external efficient exchange market when management had a *neutral* risk aversion; or an inefficient external exchange market which

favors these exposures and management has a *neutral* risk aversion. (This possibility was eliminated earlier as representing atypical imperfections in the market.)

That is, there is still one more variable, in addition to risk attitudes, which could determine the observed exposures. This is the degree of accessibility the MNC had to the domestic markets of these currencies. Exploring this factor is outside the scope of this book, so we will tentatively assume that the degree of access to these domestic markets was similar for all the currencies. This leaves us with two possible risk attitudes to explain the changes in exposure consistent with the market inefficiencies we considered typical, and no obvious explanation for the changes in exposure opposite to the ones expected from such market inefficiencies.

Test of Risk-Neutral Attitudes. A test of the prevalence of this attitude can be made by assuming that there is a relationship between the gains which could be obtained by using the domestic markets and the extent to which flows would move in the direction postulated. A ranking of the currencies by the number of quarters in table 3-4 where covered interest arbitrage, based on domestic rates, was profitable produces the following list in descending order: mark, 94 percent, invest; French franc, 68 percent, invest; pound, 68 percent, borrow; guilder, 65 percent, invest; Belgian and Swiss francs, 58 percent, invest; lira, 48 percent invest, 42 percent borrow; and Canadian dollar, 39 percent, borrow.

A comparison of this ranking of the currencies with the findings for the financing accounts reported above produces an inverse correlation. The currencies for which there was most often an incentive to take advantage of the difference between domestic and Eurorates—the German mark and the French franc—do not show most of the companies' financing accounts moving as expected. On the other hand, the other currencies, with the exception of the Canadian dollar, show the financing accounts moving in a fashion consistent with taking advantage of the market segmentation. So this test is inconclusive.

Test of Risk-Asymmetrical Attitudes. Assuming that the difficulty of having access to domestic rates was comparable in all currencies, we can test for the degree of risk asymmetry in management's decisions by measuring the reaction of financing accounts to the exposure generated by the operating accounts. Managers with a risk-asymmetrical attitude would react more strongly, with opposite movements in the financing accounts, when the operating accounts generate "undesirable" exposures than when the contrary is the case.

As described earlier, table 4-6 shows how the majority of companies had their operating accounts tending to generate positive exposures in every currency considered. Growth and the fact that most of these operations are profitable explain this tendency. However, the percentage of companies whose operating accounts generated positive exposures varied from currency to currency. This fact could influence our comparisons of the reaction of the financing accounts in different currencies, since it would bias the frequency of responses to specified types of operating exposures. Therefore, the currencies were separated into two groups: those where more than 75 percent of the companies had their operating accounts generating positive exposures and those where the percentage of companies was between 50 and 74 percent. Table 4-7 recasts the percentage of companies reporting different relationships between the financing and operating accounts in table 4-6, taking into account the two groups of currencies.

Table 4-7 shows that the financing accounts counteracted the "undesirable" exposures generated by the operating accounts more often than reinforcing this trend in every currency except the lira and the German mark. This

Table 4-7
Behavior of Financing Accounts in Relation to Exposures Generated by Operating Accounts
(*percentage of companies reporting in the given currency*)

	Changes in Financing Accounts			
	Counteracted "Undesirable" Operating Exposures	*Reinforced "Desirable" Operating Exposures*	*Counteracted "Desirable" Operating Exposures*	*Reinforced "Undesirable" Operating Exposures*
Currencies where more than 75% of companies generated "undesirable" operating exposures				
Pound	46	19	8	29
Canadian dollar	52	–	13	39
Currencies where more than 75% of companies generated "desirable" operating exposures				
French franc	12	38	42	8
Guilder	13	68	19	–
Yen	9	36	52	–
Currencies where more than 50% but less than 74% of companies generated "undesirable" operating exposures				
Lira	30	25	15	34
Currencies where more than 56% but less than 74% of the companies generated "desirable" operating exposures				
German mark	12	30	35	22
Swiss franc	31	39	15	15
Belgian franc	31	31	30	8

meant a prevalence of negative financial flows in the cases of the pound and the Canadian dollar when the operating accounts tended to generate positive exposures. In the French franc, the guilder, the yen, the Swiss franc, and the Belgian franc there was a prevalence of positive financial flows whenever the operating accounts tended to generate negative exposures. This behavior is consistent with taking advantage of market imperfections as well as having a risk-asymmetrical attitude. However, when the operating accounts generated desirable exposures, the reaction of the financing accounts was not as homogeneous. The financing accounts reinforced the desirable exposures in the cases of the pound, the guilder, the lira, the Swiss franc, and the Belgian franc; but the financing accounts tended to reduce the desirable exposures in the cases of the Canadian dollar, the French franc, the yen, and the German mark. *This difference in reaction of the financing accounts between cases when the operating accounts generate undesirable and desirable exposures supports the presence of risk-asymmetrical attitudes*, regardless of the nature of the markets.

The currencies where less than 75 percent of the companies reported the operating accounts generating positive exposures are the lira, the German mark, the Swiss franc, and the Belgian franc. In contrast to the other currencies which have a high frequency of entries under operating exposures which are positive, these other four currencies have their entries in table 4-7 more evenly distributed. Given the small sample in each group (a subset of the participating thirty-six companies), it is harder to separate the effect of the multiple factors which could interact in the decision. Significantly, the two exceptions to the expected relationship in the financing accounts occur in the lira and the German mark, two of the currencies in this group. The behavior of the financing accounts when the operating accounts generate desirable exposures does not appear to be associated with the percentage of companies reporting positive operating exposures.

Overall, an attitude of risk asymmetry toward exposure to exchange risk appears to provide a better explanation for the observed behavior in the financing accounts in different currencies. It happens that this behavior is also consistent with realizing a profit from access to domestic markets in some currencies. Whether this was also a contributing factor depends on the access of the MNCs to domestic rates. However, to the extent that access to domestic rates was similar in all currencies, this profit does not appear to have been the major factor affecting the behavior of these companies. The odds that domestic rates were more accessible in the markets where the behavior of MNCs' is consistent with taking advantage of those rates (pound, lira, Swiss franc) than in the other currencies (German mark, French franc) are rather small.

Summary

The taxonomy of possible management policies toward exchange risk developed in this chapter is based on the combination of these managers' attitude toward risk and their perceptions of the financial markets. These combinations produced six possible policies.

The search for the policy best supported by the data proceeded by elimination. Three of the possibilities were eliminated because they represented market imperfections inconsistent with the typical inefficiencies found in chapter 3. The remaining market inefficiencies, although possible in any market, are consistent with an external exchange market which is efficient. They are the inefficiencies derived from the market segmentation produced by exchange controls. For the MNC with access to domestic and external markets, exchange controls in an otherwise efficient external market make it desirable to borrow or to be short in the depreciating currencies and to invest or to be long in appreciating currencies.

Another three possibilities were eliminated by testing for the presence of a risk-paranoid attitude where any exposure to exchange risk is intolerable and therefore must be reduced to zero. The evidence is overwhelmingly against the hypothesis that companies followed a policy of constantly reducing exposures to zero.

Two more possibilities were eliminated by testing for behavior which was consistent with assuming that the financial markets were efficient. For managers with a risk-asymmetrical attitude, the exposures would be zero. Yet, in testing for the risk-paranoid position we found that a policy of reducing exposures to zero is not supported by the data. For managers with a risk-neutral attitude, exposures would be random in an efficient market. Then, if managers assumed the markets to be efficient, the resulting exposure shown in these data would have been possible only if they had a risk-neutral attitude. If the markets are disregarded because they are efficient, the exposures observed would not change sizably from quarter to quarter, except for seasonal variations. And so we tested whether the quarter-to-quarter changes in the exposures were significantly different from zero. The data show that in most cases they were. Also, if managers assume the markets to be efficient, the exposures in different currencies would be similar, since they are dictated by business operations which could be expected to be similar in different currencies. But this outcome, too, was hard to substantiate with the data. A uniform policy toward all currencies is not supported by the data. These two tests lead us to dismiss one more possible set of policies.

After the above eliminations, we were left with only two possibilities in our taxonomy. Managers must have operated on the assumption of some degree of inefficiency in the market. These inefficiencies appear to have encouraged borrowing in depreciating currencies and investing in appreciating currencies. The two possibilities left distinguish between two possible risk attitudes: risk-neutral and risk-asymmetrical.

Each company's data were segregated by account and currency. The accounts in each currency were aggregated into two groups: operating and financing accounts. The operating accounts were assumed to tend to generate exposures determined by the nature of the operations of the company. The financing accounts, on the other hand, are the ones where the financial officers had the most leverage to achieve desired exposure positions—given market and company constraints.

To the extent that a pattern emerges, financial variables tended to counteract the exposures generated by operations when this exposure was likely to generate exchange losses. This is the case in pounds and lire where the financial variables actively moved to reduce the positive exposure that operations tended to generate in those currencies. In Swiss francs, the positive movements of financial variables tend to counteract the negative average net exposure in this currency. In the other relatively strong currencies, however, operations which tended to generate positive exposures were allowed to prevail. In these currencies the financial variables did not show a definitive trend toward positive or negative exposures. However, the movement of the financial variables still left the majority of the exposures in these currencies on the positive side.

These findings support the hypothesis that management has an asymmetrical attitude toward risks in the foreign-exchange market. In some currencies this attitude was consistent with taking advantage of discrepancies between domestic and external rates. In the weak currencies, where operations were prone to generate losses, and in Swiss francs where an overall negative net exposure prevailed, strong steps were taken in the financial accounts in an attempt to counteract the undesirable exposures. On the other hand, in the stronger currencies, the movement of the financial accounts was sufficiently weak to leave the companies on the right side of exposure.

Notes

1. A preliminary version of this chapter appeared in Rita M. Rodriguez, "Management of Foreign Exchange Risk in U.S. Multinationals," *Sloan Management Review*, Spring 1978, pp. 31-49.

2. See chapter 2, the section entitled "The Variable to Be Managed: Exposure."

3. Given the small size of the sample, the "Student's t" distribution was used to test whether mean exposure for each currency and the total were statistically different from zero. Table 4-2 shows the results using a 95 percent confidence interval.

4. The objective of disregarding the sign of the changes in aggregating was to avoid the possibility of plus and minus changes canceling in the addition process. When looking at the exposure throughout time for each currency, we are interested primarily in the degree of instability in the exposure in each currency. This degree of instability is best captured if one ignores the direction

of the changes so that when these changes are summed, increases and decreases in exposure through time do not counteract one another.

5. The effectiveness of this test is limited by the fact that we are using absolute changes. The deductions presented above are correct insofar as the sign of the exposure remains constant. That is, if the exposure was positive and accounted for 25 percent of total exposure in the first period, then if the exposure remains positive and accounts for the same percentage of total exposure in the second period, one can support the theory that the currency is being treated in the same way as the total. However, suppose the sign of the exposure turns from positive to negative and the percentage of total exposure accounted for by the currency remains constant. Given that one is looking at absolute numbers, it would be wrong to conclude that the company maintains the same posture for this currency as for the total. Alternatively, after the change in sign of the exposure, if the exposure now accounts for more or less of total exposure than previously, one would be wrong to conclude that this currency necessarily is being treated differently from the total. However, the number of changes in sign of exposure from one quarter to the next is relatively small.

6. This calculation is in contrast to the preceding analysis where the objective was to obtain a measure of instability, and both positive and negative changes were pooled disregarding their signs.

7. The only significant accounts on a balance sheet omitted here are fixed assets and stockholders' equity.

8. The figures shown in table 4-6 are the result of aggregating the entries of each of the companies in the sample for each currency. However, not all companies reported in all currencies or in the same subset of currencies. That is why we find a different total number of companies accounted for in each currency in each account.

5 The Behavior of U.S. Multinational Companies during the Exchange Crises

In chapter 4 we presented evidence that the activities of the companies indicated an awareness of potential currency movements consistent with a continuous reassessment of risks and returns in the exchange markets. The conclusions of that chapter were based on the study of average behavior of each company throughout the whole period. Was this behavior also prevalent *during* the periods associated with crises in the foreign-exchange markets? These companies wield fantastic financial power. To the extent that they moved their liquid resources from one currency to another in phase with the fluctuations in the exchange markets, the fluctuations in these markets would have been aggravated.

This chapter will focus on specific periods when the international monetary system was recognized to have been in a state of turmoil. The question will be whether MNCs contributed to this turmoil.

How Can MNCs Affect the Foreign-Exchange Markets?

Any time that a manager changes the currency composition of a given or expected level of cash, this manager affects the foreign-exchange market. Any time that a manager enters into a forward-exchange contract, this manager affects the foreign-exchange market. However, from previous chapters we learned that the primary concern of management is net exposure to foreign-exchange risk. How does this concern affect the foreign-exchange markets?

Management's concern with exposure to foreign-exchange risk affects the exchange markets when the concern translates into operations in the cash account. However, net exposure includes such accounts as accounts receivable and short-term debt which usually do not involve the exchange markets. It is only when the management of these accounts is reflected in the currency composition of the cash account that exchange markets are affected. There are two ways in which MNCs can affect the foreign-exchange markets: directly and through alteration of the account composition in net exposure.

Direct Operations of MNCs in the Exchange Markets

An MNC affects the exchange markets directly when it exchanges one currency into another or when an expected currency exchange does not take place.

Take the case of an appreciating currency, and assume that the MNC wishes to increase its cash holdings in that currency. For illustration, I will use the German mark as the currency. The MNC can accomplish its goal of increasing its cash balances in German marks in one of two ways: by exchanging other currencies (say, dollars) into marks or by failing to execute a usual conversion of marks into other currencies (say, failing to declare a dividend to the parent company in marks). This is usually referred to as "lagging a payment."

In the first case, the demand for marks and the supply of dollars will increase. This is shown in figure 5-1A. The shift in the demand for marks from DD to D'D' will increase the price of marks in terms of dollars. In the second case, the expected supply of marks will not materialize. This is equivalent to a reduction in the supply of marks. In figure 5-1B this is shown by the shift of the supply curve from SS to S'S'. The impact of this shift is also an increase in the price of marks in terms of dollars.

The MNC in our example can also achieve its objective of increasing holdings of German marks through the forward exchange market. The company can enter a forward contract to purchase German marks against dollars for

Part A   An Increase in Demand for Marks

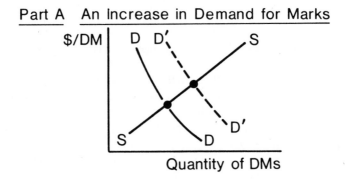

Quantity of DMs

Part B   A Decrease in Supply of Marks

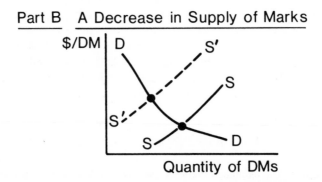

Quantity of DMs

Figure 5-1. Impact of MNCs on Foreign-Exchange Markets.

delivery in three months at a predetermined rate—the forward rate. When the contract matures, the company's holdings of marks increase and the holdings of dollars decrease. If the exchange markets are in equilibrium, the operation in the forward market is equivalent to purchasing German marks with dollars in the spot market and investing the proceeds in a three-month security denominated in marks. However, when using the forward market, the MNC's direct pressure on the spot rate is delayed until the forward contract matures.

In the case of a weakening currency, let's say the pound, in which the MNC tries to decrease its liquid holdings by operating in the spot market, it can follow one of two alternatives: it can exchange the pound into other currencies (say, dollars), or it can advance the timing of a planned conversion of pounds into other currencies (for example, prepaying an account payable). This is usually referred to as "leading a payment." The MNC could also sell pounds against other currency in the forward market. The result of these transactions will tend to reduce the price of the weakening currency against other currencies. In terms of the figure, the supply of the weakening currency will increase, and expected demand for the currency will fail to materialize.

Impact of Exposure Management on Exchange Markets

Changing the level of any of the accounts included in the definition of net exposure will affect the net exposure only if the currency composition of the liquid asset accounts also is changed. One can think of operations designed to change the net exposure in a currency as taking place in two steps. In the first step only the account composition of the net exposure changes. In the second step the level of net exposure changes.

Assume the case of a weakening currency. In this case, an MNC will want to do the following in that currency:

1. Decrease the level of accounts receivable;
2. Decrease the level of inventory, if this is considered exposed;
3. Increase the level of borrowing;
4. Increase the level of accounts payable.

The result of each of these transactions will be to increase the level of cash in the weakening currency. To change the net exposure in that currency calls for one further step: The cash balances generated from these transactions must be exchanged into harder currencies.[1] Otherwise, the company would have succeeded in changing only the account composition of its exposure in the weakening currency, not the level of the net exposure. It is at this point, when the cash balances in one currency are exchanged into another currency, that the MNC affects the exchange markets directly as well as the level of its net exposure.

Lag between Changes in Account Composition in Net
Exposure and the Impact in the Exchange Markets

How much time does usually elapse between the preparatory changes in the account composition of net exposure and the actual transfer of funds in the exchange market? This lag depends on the geographical location of the party accomplishing the change in the account composition—inside or outside the home country of the currency in question—and on the controls on foreign-exchange transactions within the country governing the given currency.

In general, if the party accomplishing the first step in changing the net exposure (changing the account composition) is located outside the home country of the currency, the exchange from the weak currency into a stronger currency can take place almost immediately. On the other hand, if the party changing the account composition of net exposure is located within the boundaries of the government regulating the given currency, the final transfer of funds may be delayed since the foreign-exchange controls are likely to act as a deterrent to such a transfer.

To illustrate the previous point, consider the case of an account receivable denominated in a weakening currency. Assume that the MNC has succeeded in collecting this account receivable which was denominated in lire. If the receivable was owned by a party outside Italy, the lira proceeds from the collection process will most likely be exchanged into a harder currency almost immediately. After all, this transfer was the ultimate objective of the company in reducing its level of accounts receivable in lire. On the other hand, if the owner of the receivable was a subsidiary located inside Italy, the company must face a further hurdle. The lira proceeds must be exchanged into a harder currency. However, in order to accomplish this task, the foreign-exchange controls which Italy imposes on this type of transaction must be observed. These controls may make it impossible to accomplish the eventual transfer of funds and therefore to change the level of net exposure in lire.

Even when the company does not succeed in transferring the lira proceeds into a harder currency, the MNC is affecting the foreign-exchange markets indirectly. The excess liquidity created inside Italy constitutes a potential demand for foreign currency against the lira. If the controls are eliminated or reduced in scope, these funds will promptly find their way into the exchange market.

The empirical research presented in the following sections analyzes both cash and noncash items, that is, accounts which do not affect the exchange markets directly. The presumption is that a transfer into other currencies is possible, or that the changes by themselves increase exchange-market pressures in terms of government-suppressed supply or demand, even if the actual exchange is not consummated.

Empirical Evidence

Measuring the Evidence

The behavior of the thirty-six companies studied in the previous chapter is analyzed in this chapter during selected periods identified as crisis periods. The accounts studied are the same as before: net exposure and the component accounts. The basic types of measurements for each company are also the same as those used in chapter 4: average levels and quarter-to-quarter percentage changes. However, instead of including the whole period, 1967 to 1974, these measurements are now taken for short periods, with one and two quarters around a date marking an exchange crisis period.

For each crisis period three summary statistics were computed for each currency in each company: the average level of the account, the average value of the positive percentage changes, and the average value of the negative percentage changes. The data for each company were then pooled. In this pooling the account levels assign heavier weight to the large companies when the levels are aggregated. However, the percentage changes make it possible to give the same weight to the data from each company.

The periods of crisis in the foreign-exchange markets during which the changes in the MNC accounts were measured are centered on the following dates and events:

June 1971   Several European currencies are upvalued, and the German mark is allowed to float in value in the foreign-exchange markets.

December 1971   The Smithsonian Agreement establishes new parities for major currencies against the U.S. dollar. These rates are well above the rates existing in August 1971 when the value of the U.S. dollar was allowed to float.

June 1972   The pound sterling is allowed to float (and sink) in the exchange markets.

March 1973   This date is the end of a quarter that began with the upvaluation of the Swiss franc and the Japanese yen, leading to the devaluation of the U.S. dollar against the major currencies. The attacks on the U.S. dollar started again in March.

June 1973   After a short period of tranquillity in April and May, upvaluations of the major European currencies against the U.S. dollar occurred throughout the summer of 1973.

Although the climaxes of the specific crisis periods did not always occur at the end of a calendar quarter, as the benchmark dates suggest, the company data were collected on this basis. This fact constrained the selection of the critical periods. Given the relatively short period covered by each observation and the a priori uncertainty as to the climax of the crisis, this inaccuracy should not bias the analysis.[2]

As in chapter 4, the currencies for each observed period were divided into two groups: those appreciating against the U.S. dollar (the French franc, the German mark, the Swiss franc, the guilder, the Belgian franc, and the yen) and those currencies constant or depreciating against the U.S. dollar (the lira, the pound, the Canadian dollar, and the U.S. dollar itself). Except for the June 1972 crisis, which was mainly a pound devaluation crisis, the major contribution of this grouping of currencies is to segregate the data for strongly appreciating currencies from the other currencies. The sample data for less strong currencies include fewer observations than the sample for appreciating currencies. Also, to the extent that the movement in the strong currencies was almost monotonic, probably there was more incentive *to take advantage of* movements in the stronger currencies than in the weaker ones. This is in contrast to the behavior *to protect* the company against undesirable exposures discussed in chapter 4.

In summary, the preparation of each company's exposure data in the manner just described provides six measures for the pooled data:

1. Average level of the account in strong currencies.
2. Average level of the account in weak currencies.
3. Average of positive percentage changes in the strong currencies.
4. Average of positive percentage changes in the weak currencies.
5. Average of negative percentage changes in the strong currencies.
6. Average of negative percentage changes in the weak currencies.

These measures are provided for each account of interest for each period observed around a benchmark date. These figures are presented in appendix 5A.

Testing the Consistency of MNC Behavior with
Exchange-Market Movements

A rationality characterized by the MNCs moving their funds in sympathy with the exchange markets would have the companies holding more assets in appreciating currencies than in depreciating ones and increasing their holdings of assets in appreciating currencies while decreasing debt in those currencies. In terms of the accounts analyzed in this book, the following flows in appreciating currencies could be expected:

1. Increase in the holdings of cash and marketable securities, accounts receivable, inventory, and purchases of forward foreign-exchange contracts.
2. Decrease in short-term debt, accounts payable, long-term debt, and sales of forward-exchange contracts.
3. Movement toward a more positive or less negative net exposure position.

In terms of the measurements discussed in the preceding section, MNCs would be moving funds in the same direction as the trends in the exchange markets if those movements achieved the following for asset accounts:

1. Average level of the account for strong currencies is larger than the average level for weak currencies.
2. Average of positive percentage changes in strong currencies is larger than the average negative percentage change in those currencies.
3. Average of positive percentage changes in weak currencies is less than the average negative percentage change in those currencies.
4. Average of positive percentage changes in strong currencies is larger than in weak currencies.
5. Average of negative percentage changes in strong currencies is less than in weak currencies.

For liability accounts the opposite relationships would be postulated.

The presence of the postulated relationships, as well as the opposite ones, is summarized in table 5-1. In the *headings* of this table strong currencies are indicated by an S and weak currencies by a W. The direction of change is noted by arrows; upward arrows denote positive changes, and downward arrows indicate negative changes. There are no arrows at the head of the first column on the left because that column refers to the comparison of the average *levels* of the account between strong and weak currencies.

The *body* of the table indicates whether the relationship between the given numbers is as postulated. If it is, the outcome is called a right (R) one; if not, the outcome is called a wrong (W) one. The four columns in each sequence of comparisons indicate, from left to right, the comparisons for (1) Two quarters before the benchmark date, (2) One quarter before the benchmark date, (3) One quarter after the benchmark date, and (4) Two quarters after the benchmark date. The asterisk accompanying some of the letters indicates those relationships which were significant at a 95 percent confidence level.

Accounts Affecting the Exchange Market Directly. The previous discussion indicates that to assess the impact of MNCs on the foreign-exchange markets, one should look at their liquid balances and their operations in the forward-exchange market. Table 5-1 shows the comparisons for levels and changes in these two accounts around the benchmark dates.

Table 5-1
Account Levels and Changes: Relationships between Strong and Weak Currencies Compared during Foreign-Exchange Crises

	Level Level S > W				↑S > ↑W				↓S < ↓W				↑S > ↓S				↑W < ↓W			
	1	2	3	4	1	2	3	4	1	2	3	4	1	2	3	4	1	2	3	4
Assets — Cash																				
June 1971	R*	R*	R*	R*	W	W*	R	R	R	R	W	W	R*	R	R*	R	W	W*	W*	W*
December 1971	R*	R*	R*	R*	R	R	R	W	R	W*	W*	W	R	R	R	R*	W	R	W	W*
June 1972	W*	W	W*	W*	R	R	R	R	–	W	R	W	R*	R*	R*	R*	W*	W*	W	W*
March 1973	R*	R*	R*	R*	R	R	R	R	R*	R	W	R	R*	W*	R	R	W	R*	W*	W
June 1973	R*	R*	R*	R*	R	R	R	R	R	R	R	R	R	R	R	R	R	W	R	W
Forward Contracts																				
June 1971	W*	W*	W*	W*	W*	–	W	W	–	–	–	W	–	–	–	–	R	–	R	R
December 1971	W*	W*	W*	R*	W	W	W	–	–	–	R	R	–	–	R	R*	R	R	W	–
June 1972	R*	R*	W*	R*	R	R*	R*	R	W	–	–	–	R	–	R	R	W	R	R	R
March 1973	R	R*	R*	R*	W*	W*	W	W	–	R	–	R	–	R	–	R	R	R	R	R*
June 1973	R*	R*	R*	R*	W	W	R	W	R	–	R	R	R	R	R	R	R	R	R	W
Accounts Receivable																				
June 1971	W*	W*	W*	W*	W*	W*	R	R	–	W	W	W*	R	–	R	R	W	W*	W	W*
December 1971	R*	W*	W*	W	R	R	R	R	W*	W*	–	W	R	R	R	R	W	W	R	W
June 1972	W*	W*	W*	W*	R	R	W	R	W*	W	W	W*	R	W	W	R	W	W	W	W*
March 1973	W*	W*	W*	W*	R	R	R	W	W*	W	R	–	R	W	R	R*	W*	R	W	W
June 1973	W*	W	W*	W*	R	R	R	W	W	R	W	R	R	R	R	R	W*	W	R	W
Inventory																				
June 1971	W*	W*	W*	W*	W	W	W	R*	W	W	–	–	W	W	R	R*	W	W	W	W
December 1971	W*	W*	W*	W*	R*	R	W	R	W	–	–	R*	R*	W*	–	R	W*	W*	W	R
June 1972	W*	W*	W*	W*	R	W	W*	R	R*	–	R*	R	R*	R	R*	R	W*	W*	W	R*
March 1973	W*	W	W*	W*	R	R	W	W	W	–	–	W	R*	R*	–	R	W	R*	W	W*
June 1972	W*	W*	W*	W*	R	W	W	W	–	W	–	–	R	–	–	R	–	W	W	W

Liabilities

Short-Term Debt

June 1971	R*	R*	R	R*	W	—	W	R	W	W	W*	W	R	R	R*	R
December 1971	R	R*	R*	R*	R	R	W	W	W	W	W	W*	R	R	W	W
June 1972	R*	R*	R*	W*	W*	W	—	W	W*	W*	W	W	R*	R*	W	W*
March 1973	R*	W*	W*	W*	—	R	W	W*	W	W*	W	W*	R*	W	R	R
June 1973	W	W*	W*	W*	—	W	W*	W	W	W	W	W	R*	R	—	W

Long-Term Debt

June 1971	R*	R*	R*	R*	R	W	W	—	R	W	W	W	—	R	R	W
December 1971	R*	R*	R*	R*	W*	R	R	W	R	R	W	W	R	R	R	W
June 1972	R*	R*	R*	W*	R	—	—	—	W	W	W	—	R	W	—	W*
March 1973	W*	W*	W*	W*	—	R	R	W	W	W	W	W*	—	W	R	R
June 1973	W*	W*	W*	W*	R	R	W	W	R	W*	W*	W	R	R	—	W

Accounts Payable

June 1971	R*	R*	R*	R*	W	W	W	W	W	W	W	W*	W	W	—	R*
December 1971	W*	R*	R*	R*	W	W*	W*	R	R	W	W	W*	W*	R	R	R
June 1972	R*	R*	R*	W*	—	R	R	W	W*	W	W	W*	R	R	R*	R
March 1973	R*	R*	R*	R*	R	R	W	R*	W	R*	R	W	R	R	R*	R*
June 1973	R*	R*	R*	R*	W	W*	W	W*	R	R	R	W	R	W	W	W

Company definition of exposure plus forward contracts

June 1971	W*	W*	W*	W*	R	W	W	W	W	R	W	W	W	R	W	W
December 1971	W*	W*	W*	W*	W	R	R	R	W	W	W	W	W	W	W	W
June 1972	W*	W*	W*	W*	W	R	R	W	R	R	R	W	R	R	R	R
March 1973	R*	R*	R*	R	W	W	W	R	W	W	R*	R	W	R	R	R
June 1973	W*	W	W*	R*	R	R	R	W	R	W	W	W	R	W	R	W

Source: Appendix 5A.

↑ = increase; ↓ = decrease.

S = Strong currencies: Belgian franc, French franc, German mark, guilder, Swiss franc, and yen.

W = Weak currencies: Canadian dollar, lira, and pound.

*The "Student's t" distribution was used to test whether the differences between the strong and weak currencies were significantly different from zero. All relationships marked with an asterisk were found to be significant at a 95% confidence level.

Column headings: 1: two quarters before the benchmark date; 2: one quarter before the benchmark date; 3: one quarter after the benchmark date; 4: two quarters after the benchmark date.

R = Right outcome. Relationship between strong and weaker currencies is as postulated.

W = Wrong outcome. Relationship between strong and weaker currencies is opposite to the one postulated.

The *cash account* presents a very vivid picture in which MNCs succeeded in maintaining higher levels of liquid balances in strong currencies than in weak currencies. This success can be traced to the consistently large increases, relative to decreases, in holdings of strong currencies. Although the holdings of weak currencies also increased (positive changes in weak currencies are also larger than negative changes in those currencies), the average positive increase in strong currencies was usually larger than the average increase in weak currencies. In spite of the bias introduced by the fact that the level of strong currencies was greater than that of weak currencies (therefore tending to make percentage changes in strong currencies smaller than for weak currencies), the data show positive percentage changes in strong currencies to be larger than in weak currencies.[3] *The companies in every crisis period were accumulating liquid holdings of strong currencies at a faster rate than holdings of weak currencies.* As a consequence, on the average, their holdings of strong currencies were larger than for weak currencies. The one exception to the case of holding larger balances in strong currencies than in weak currencies occurs around the June 1972 benchmark. In these computations the currencies considered to be weak remain the same for all benchmarks; however, during 1972 the only currency that was clearly weak was the pound sterling. After the Smithsonian Agreement in Devember 1971, a certain degree of calm returned to the exchange markets with the exception of the pound sterling in the second quarter of 1972. Under these conditions, it would not be surprising if the MNCs, which had been restraining the increase in the so-called weak currencies during 1971,then allowed the balances in the previously weaker currencies to increase to more normal levels during 1972. Consistent with this hypothesis is the fact that for the two comparisons preceding June 1972 one finds that the increase in cash holdings in what I call weak currencies was significantly larger than the decrease in these currencies. Also the decrease in cash holdings in what I call weak currencies was smaller than the decrease for strong currencies at that time.

The paucity of data on *forward contracts* makes it difficult to reach any conclusion. However, with the exception of the comparisons around June 1971, these companies had forward purchases exceeding sales in strong currencies, while the opposite was true for weak currencies. This finding in the level of outstanding contracts is substantiated by the comparisons of changes. Positive changes (forward purchases) were always larger than negative changes (forward sales) in strong currencies. That is, increases in long positions or reductions in short positions in strong currencies were larger than the decreases in long positions or increase in short positions in those currencies. For weak currencies the tendency appears to be for increases in short positions or decreases in long positions.

The two accounts in which the impact of MNCs on foreign-exchange markets is reflected directly, cash and forward contracts, show that these companies were moving their funds with the tides in that market during every foreign-exchange crisis. They accumulated funds and maintained long positions in forward contracts in strong currencies to a much larger degree than in weaker currencies.

Other Current Assets. Accounts receivable and inventory are the two other current asset accounts included in this study. In chapter 4 these accounts were associated with the level of operations of the business instead of the considerations of a purely financial nature. Table 5-1 shows that whatever impact financial considerations may have had on the level of these accounts, these considerations did not succeed in producing larger balances in strong currencies than in weak currencies. Actually, with almost no exception, the opposite appears to be the case: the levels of weak currencies in these accounts are significantly higher than the levels in strong currencies.

It is true that the increases in receivables and inventory denominated in strong currencies were often larger than the decreases in these currencies, but this was also the case for weak currencies. General growth in business operations made the level of the accounts increase more often and by larger amounts than it would decrease. When one looks for further evidence in comparing the size of the increases in strong currencies with the size of increases in weak currencies, one finds a large majority of right outcomes in the case of accounts receivable. However, the pattern is mixed for inventories.

Apparently, the nature of the operations of these businesses produced higher levels for these two accounts in weak currencies than in strong currencies. In the case of accounts receivable there appears to be an undercurrent to change this situation by having the increases in strong currencies larger than the decreases in those currencies and larger than the increases in weak currencies. However, in spite of these trends, the majority of the accounts receivable remained denominated in weak currencies.

In the case of the inventory account I can find no distinguishable trend to move a larger proportion of this account into harder currency. The motivation for this action would be one more excuse to have resources denominated in stronger currencies. However, the cash flow derived from the sale of inventory is determined by the currency in which the sale is denominated. It is true that to the extend that inventory is sold locally, the sales will usually be invoiced in terms of the local currency. However, some of this inventory will be exported. In this latter case the currency of invoicing is not necessarily the same as that of the location of the inventory. Also, often the accounting system used by these companies divided the inventory account of foreign subsidiaries between local and dollar inventory. The dollar content of the inventory was usually the portion bought from the parent company or from another subsidiary. The assumption behind this practice is that in case of a devaluation of the local currency, the imported content of inventory could be sold at a higher local price. That is, local regulations will exempt imports from any potential controls on local prices. To the extent that this practice has been followed by the companies, the balances in weak currencies, including the dollar, will tend to be larger.

Liabilities. There are three liability accounts in this study: accounts payable, short-term debt, and long-term debt. In all there is a tendency for the average level of weak currencies to be higher than the average level of the accounts in strong currencies. Also, there is a tendency for the increases in weak currencies to be larger than the decreases in those currencies. However, the positive changes in strong currencies are also larger than the negative changes in those currencies. In general, these data show the weaker currencies providing a larger amount and an increasing proportion of total financing.

In the case of accounts payable, increases in weaker currencies were larger than in stronger currencies in most instances. The one exception, as shown in table 5-1, is the comparison for June 1971, where the opposite is found. Given that the level of weak currencies in accounts payable is larger than in strong currencies, there is a bias to make percentage changes in weak currencies appear smaller than in strong currencies. My findings show the increases in weak currencies to be larger than in strong currencies in spite of this bias.

For the two borrowing accounts, short- and long-term debt, note that for the last two benchmarks the general relationship between the level of debt in strong and weak currencies is reversed. For the comparisons around March and June 1973, the average level of borrowings is larger in strong currencies than in weak currencies. This is in contrast to the comparison for the preceding benchmarks where the opposite relationship prevailed. This is surprising, given that by 1973 the so-called strong currencies were much more recognized for their strength than they had been in earlier periods. However, this possible increase in recognition took place not only among the MNCs but also in the financial markets. To the extent that the lenders prevailed in these transactions, they would have preferred to lend in strong currencies. This preference on the part of lenders, coupled with the lower interest rates associated with loans in the stronger currencies, appears to have switched the larger proportion of the borrowings by these companies from the relatively weak currencies to the relatively strong ones during late 1972 and 1973.

As mentioned before, borrowings in both strong and weak currencies had large increases relative to the decreases. However, when comparing the size of the increases in weak currencies with those in strong currencies, I usually find that increases in debt in strong currencies are larger than increases in weak currencies. It is true that in this case the bias introduced by comparing two percentage numbers with different bases will tend to produce smaller percentage changes for weak currencies. However, when comparing the decreases in strong currencies with those in weak currencies, I also find a mixed pattern. This piece of information, together with the fact that during the last two benchmarks the level of borrowings in strong currencies was larger than in weak currencies, seems to indicate that borrowing in strong currency increased faster than it did in weak currencies.

To the extent that companies tried to manage the currency composition of their liabilities to take advantage of fluctuations in the exchange markets, they appear to have been more successful in accomplishing this goal through accounts payable than through borrowings. Borrowing levels had the anticipated relationship between the levels in strong and weak currencies until mid-1972, but not afterward. The relationship between increases in strong and weak currencies also supports the above summary statement.[4]

It is interesting to contrast the findings for accounts payable with those for accounts receivable. Table 5-1 shows that the levels as well as the changes in accounts receivable did not conform to expectations based on the performance of the exchange market. However, we have just seen that accounts payable resembles the expected behavior rather closely. Thus, it appears that in trade transactions these buyers had more bargaining power in the determination of the currency of invoicing and the maturity of the payment than the sellers did.

Conduits for Changing the Cash Position

The specific ways in which the MNCs affect the foreign-exchange markets have implications for policymakers who try to regulate these cash flows. The preceding section showed that the average holdings of liquid funds for the sample companies were higher in strong currencies than in weak currencies in every single crisis period. This behavior tended to perpetuate itself as the companies accumulated cash in strong currencies faster than in weak currencies in every crisis. The impact of these cash flows on the foreign-exchange market depends on the conduits used to achieve them.

The increase in holdings of strong currencies could have happened in two main ways: by a transfer of balances from weak currencies into strong currencies and by internal funds generated in strong currencies. The first source could contribute when the proceeds of borrowings in weak currencies were converted into strong currencies. It could also contribute when balances generated internally in weak currencies were converted to strong currencies. The second source of holdings in strong currencies would be merchandise sales in those currencies. To establish which one of these two approaches was most prevalent, we will relate the behavior of the balance sheet accounts studied to the changes in the cash account.

Table 5-2 summarizes the typical relationships observed between changes in strong and weak currencies for each account studied during the five crisis periods. In the case of comparisons between *levels* in strong and weak currencies, the impact on the cash account takes place in the future as the accounts are liquidated. In the case of comparisons between the *changes* in strong and weak currencies, the impact on the cash account took place in the past. As each of these accounts changes in level, it constitutes a source or a use of funds.

To establish the source of the changes in the cash accounts, I will segregate the accounts into the two groups used in chapter 4: financing and operating

Table 5-2
Typical Relationships in Account Levels and Changes during
Foreign-Exchange Crises

	Comparisons between						
	Levels			Changes			
Financing Accounts							
Cash	S	>	W	↑S	>	↑W	
Forward contracts	S	>	W	↑S	>	↑W	
Short-term debt	S	<	W[a]	↑S	>	↑W	
Long-term debt	S	<	W[b]	↑S	=	↑W	
Operating Accounts							
Accounts receivable	S	<	W	↑S	>	↑W	
Inventory	S	<	W	↑S	=	↑W	
Accounts payable	S	<	W	↑S	<	↑W	

S = Strong currencies: Belgian franc, French franc, German mark, guilder, Swiss franc, and yen.
W = Weak currencies: Canadian dollar, lira, and pound.

[a]Until March 1973; afterward the relationship is reversed.

[b]Until September 1972; afterward the relationship is reversed.

accounts. In this fashion we should be able to detect whether the changes in the cash account originated in internal operations or in financial transactions in the capital markets. The impact of the typical behavior of the accounts on the cash accounts is shown in table 5-3.

The upper part of table 5-3 shows the impact on cash balances implicit in the relationship between levels in strong and weak currencies. This implicit relationship is realized when the accounts are liquidated. This is one of the two elements measured by the change comparisons, as discussed below.

The *changes* in the accounts studied are composed of two parts: liquidation of initial balances and addition of new balances. For example, in accounts receivables the observed changes are due to collection of outstanding receivables and addition of new receivables. Since my objective is to establish the flows between strong and weak currencies, it is necessary to associate a dominant type of currency with each component of change. In table 5-3 I associate the liquidation of previously outstanding balances with the type of currency prevalent in the comparison of *levels* of the two types of currencies. I associate the addition of new balances with the currency prevalent in the comparison of *changes* in the two types of currencies.

Table 5-3 shows the likely and unlikely sources of the observed accumulation of cash in strong currencies:

1. Borrowings in short- and long-term debt contributed to the accumulation of cash in strong currencies only inasmuch as in an earlier period

Table 5-3

Impact of Accounts' Typical Behavior on Cash Account during Foreign-Exchange Crises

Comparison of Levels		Impact on Cash Account
Financing Accounts		
Short-term debt:	$S < W^a$	Levels in earlier crises indicate larger future consumption
Long-term debt:	$S < W$	of weak currencies than strong currencies as payments are made. In later crises these accounts will require more strong currencies to repay the debt.
Operating Accounts		
Accounts receivable	$S < W$	Will generate more weak currencies than strong currencies
Inventory	$S < W$	in the future as collections of receivables are made.
Accounts payable	$S < W$	Will consume more weak currencies than strong currencies in the future as payments are made.

Comparison of Changes		Liquidation of Outstanding Balances	Addition of New Balances
Financing Accounts			
Short-term debt	$\uparrow S > \uparrow W^a$	Uses more weak currencies than strong currencies during earlier crises. During later crises uses more strong currencies.	Generates more strong currencies than weak ones.
Long-term debt	$\uparrow S = \uparrow W^b$	Mixed	Mixed
Operating Accounts			
Accounts receivable	$\uparrow S > \uparrow W$	Generates more weak currencies than strong ones.	*Will* generate more strong currencies than weak ones in the future.
Inventory	$\uparrow S = \uparrow W$	Depends on currency of eventual sale.	
Accounts payable	$\uparrow S > \uparrow W$	Uses more weak currencies than strong ones.	*Will* require more weak currencies than strong ones in the future.

S = Strong currencies: Belgian franc, French franc, German mark, guilder, Swiss franc, and yen.
W = Weak currencies: Canadian dollar, lira, and pound.

[a]Until March 1973; afterward the relationship is reversed.

[b]Until September 1972; afterward the relationship is reversed.

repayment of debt required more weak currency than strong currency. However, the conventional use of the money market to alter net exposure is not supported by these data. These companies were not increasing their short-term borrowings in weak currencies to exchange them for holdings of harder currencies. To the contrary, these companies more often than not increased their borrowings in strong currencies, not weak ones. Increases in long-term debt were as often in strong as in weak currencies.

2. Internal funds tended to be generated more in weak currencies than in strong currencies. However, certain portions must have been generated in the stronger currencies. Internally generated funds could appear in the form of increased holdings of strong currencies in two fashions: the funds generated

in weak currencies were converted into strong currencies; and the funds generated in strong currencies remained in those currencies.

We can corroborate the suggestions just made as to the treatment of internally generated funds by MNCs by referring to the findings of chapter 4. In that chapter I showed that operations tended to generate positive exposures and that MNCs were much more prone to try to alter this exposure when the exposure referred to a weak currency. In such cases, particularly those of the lira and the pound, the so-called financing accounts were managed in an attempt to counteract the unwanted positive exposure in those currencies.

In this chapter the data show that borrowings other than accounts payable were not major contributors to the accumulation of liquid holdings in hard currencies. Besides borrowings, the other two accounts in the financing group of accounts are cash and forward contracts. Thus, when companies were managing their financing accounts to counteract the undesirable exposures, they were transferring excess funds into strong currencies.

Summary

Multinational companies can affect the exchange markets directly and indirectly. They can affect the markets directly either by transacting in the markets or by abstaining from entering into expected transactions. The indirect impact on the foreign-exchange markets occurs as these companies change the account composition of their net exposure, thus affecting the liquidity in the given currency when a change in liquidity from an expected exchange transaction fails to materialize because of government exchange controls. Restricted forces affect the exchange markets indirectly.

Given the findings of the larger holdings of liquid funds in strong currencies than in weak currencies, we can summarize the impact of MNCs on the foreign-exchange markets during periods of crises in these markets as follows:

1. MNCs affected the exchange markets directly by converting funds generated in weak currencies into strong currencies and failing to convert funds generated in strong currencies into weak ones.
2. MNCs may have affected the foreign-exchange markets indirectly to the extent that there was a tendency to generate funds internally in weak currencies and an apparent desire to convert these funds into strong currencies. If these desires were frustrated by exchange controls, indirect pressure on the exchange markets was generated by these companies.
3. MNCs did not affect the foreign-exchange markets through the money markets, that is, by borrowing in weak currencies and investing in harder currencies.

Notes

1. The alternative ignored here is to invest the cash in a nonexposed account such as fixed assets, a policy which is usually not practical!

2. It has been argued that to see the true cash movements of a company, one would need daily, and even intraday, data. I think this may be the case if one wishes to analyze the behavior of an exchange trader. However, none of the companies interviewed perceived itself as a trader in the market, nor did it appear willing to behave as one.

3. There are potential problems in these comparisons. The comparison of dollar-equivalent values for strong and weak currencies could be biased by the implicit larger weight given to companies with a larger size. To the extent that size influences companies' behavior, the comparison of dollar-equivalent levels will be affected by this fact. However, the analysis of time series for individual companies did not show any behavioral pattern which could be explained in terms of the size of the foreign operations of the companies in the sample.

The other difficulty in the data in table 5-1 arises when percentage changes are compared. The use of percentage changes allocates the same weight to each company in the sample. However, the base used to compute each percentage change is the level of the currency in question. Given that I divide the currencies into strong and weak currencies, the base for each group of currencies at one point in time is different. Thus, when comparing positive and negative changes among strong currencies, I am comparing percentages with the same base. However, when comparing the positive changes in strong currencies with the positive changes in weak currencies, I am using a base which is different in the computation of each of the two percentage figures. However, the bias introduced by the difference in the bases of the percentages is somewhat self-correcting. For example, consider the case of an asset account where the level of the strong currencies is significantly higher than for the weak currencies. In this situation both the positive and the negative percentage changes computed for the strong currencies, the ones with the larger base, will tend to be smaller than for the weak currencies, the ones with the smaller base. Thus, when we compare the positive increases in strong currencies with positive increases in weak currencies, the bias will tend to produce a wrong outcome. On the other hand, when we compare the negative percentage changes in strong currencies with the negative percentage changes in weak currencies, the bias operates in the other direction, and it will tend to produce a right outcome. In any case, in the analysis below, I will take into account the direction of the bias in each of the comparisons.

4. These findings are consistent with those reported by the staff of the Subcommittee on Multinational Corporations for the period January through March 1973. See staff report prepared for the use of the Subcommittee on Multinational Corporations of the Committee on Foreign Relations, U.S. Senate, *Multinational Corporations in the Dollar Devaluation Crisis: Report on a Questionnaire* (Washington, D.C., June 1975).

Appendix 5A
Account Behavior
around Exchange Crises

Table 5A-1

Average Levels and Average Percentage Changes in Accounts in Appreciating versus Depreciating Currencies; Benchmark Date: June 1971

	One Preceding Quarter		One Succeeding Quarter	
	Appreciating Currencies	*Depreciating Currencies*	*Appreciating Currencies*	*Depreciating Currencies*
Cash				
Average level of account	$634,000	$526,000	$786,000	$655,000
Average value of positive changes/currency	88%	175%	74%	22%
Average value of negative changes/currency	5%	13%	11%	9%
Forward Contracts				
Average level of account	−$4,466,000	−$343,000	−$4,342,000	−$250,000
Average value of positive changes/currency	−	4%	2%	4%
Average value of negative changes/currency	−	4%	−	6%
Accounts Receivable				
Average level of account	$2,946,000	$5,241,000	$2,926,000	$4,769,000
Average value of positive changes/currency	4%	23%	7%	5%
Average value of negative changes/currency	4%	3%	5%	4%
Inventory				
Average level of account	$3,314,000	$4,129,000	$3,343,000	$4,305,000
Average value of positive changes/currency	2%	21%	9%	3%
Average value of negative changes/currency	3%	2%	2%	2%
Accounts Payable				
Average level of account	$2,118,000	$4,011,000	$2,145,000	$3,310,000
Average value of positive changes/currency	10%	5%	7%	6%
Average value of negative changes/currency	6%	10%	4%	6%
Short-Term Debt				
Average level of account	$3,076,000	$4,244,000	$3,334,000	$4,206,000
Average value of positive changes/currency	11%	10%	27%	15%
Average value of negative changes/currency	7%	7%	3%	5%

Table 5A-1 Continued

	One Preceding Quarter		One Succeeding Quarter	
	Appreciating Currencies	Depreciating Currencies	Appreciating Currencies	Depreciating Currencies
Long-Term Debt				
Average level of account	$5,303,000	$16,384,000	$5,168,000	$21,491,000
Average value of positive changes/currency	6%	2%	22%	7%
Average value of negative changes/currency	6%	1%	1%	2%
Company Definition of Exposure				
Average level of account	−$767,000	$835,000	−$755,000	$735,000
Average value of positive changes/currency	16%	6%	14%	23%
Average value of negative changes/currency	7%	10%	48%	6%

Note: Appreciating or strong currencies: Belgian franc, French franc, German mark, guilder, Swiss franc, and yen.
Depreciating or weak currencies: U.S. dollar, Canadian dollar, lira, and pound.

Table 5A-2
Average Levels and Average Percentage Changes in Accounts in Appreciating versus Depreciating Currencies; Benchmark Date: December 1971

	One Preceding Quarter		One Succeeding Quarter	
	Appreciating Currencies	Depreciating Currencies	Appreciating Currencies	Depreciating Currencies
Cash				
Average level of account	$1,365,000	$906,000	$1,935,000	$701,000
Average value of positive changes/currency	74%	45%	41%	16%
Average value of negative changes/currency	9%	7%	8%	6%
Forward Contracts				
Average level of account	−$8,695,000	$181,000	$5,655,000	$1,186,000
Average value of positive changes/currency	10%	18%	11%	11%
Average value of negative changes/currency	—	24%	6%	10%
Accounts Receivable				
Average level of account	$2,813,000	$4,285,000	$3,012,000	$4,340,000
Average value of positive changes/currency	12%	8%	122%	3%
Average value of negative changes/currency	10%	3%	6%	6%

Table 5A-2 Continued

	One Preceding Quarter		One Succeeding Quarter	
	Appreciating Currencies	*Depreciating Currencies*	*Appreciating Currencies*	*Depreciating Currencies*
Inventory				
Average level of account	$5,452,000	$6,787,000	$5,788,000	$6,710,000
Average value of positive changes/currency	7%	5%	3%	4%
Average value of negative changes/currency	2%	2%	3%	3%
Accounts Payable				
Average level of account	$3,816,000	$3,045,000	$4,161,000	$4,329,000
Average value of positive changes/currency	14%	20%	11%	41%
Average value of negative changes/currency	5%	5%	4%	13%
Short-Term Debt				
Average level of account	$2,882,000	$3,676,000	$3,776,000	$7,457,000
Average value of positive changes/currency	33%	9%	15%	6%
Average value of negative changes/currency	8%	5%	6%	8%
Long-Term Debt				
Average level of account	$6,891,000	$11,905,000	$9,057,000	$11,153,000
Average value of positive changes/currency	5%	29%	8%	10%
Average value of negative changes/currency	3%	7%	5%	1%
Company Definition of Exposure				
Average level of account	−$1,495,000	$689,000	−$2,925,000	$134,000
Average value of positive changes/currency	19%	46%	14%	6%
Average value of negative changes/currency	42%	43%	270%	174%

Note: Appreciating or strong currencies: Belgian franc, French franc, German mark, guilder, Swiss franc, and yen.

Depreciating or weak currencies: U.S. dollar, Canadian dollar, lira, and pound.

Table 5A-3
Average Levels and Average Percentage Changes in Accounts in Appreciating versus Depreciating Currencies; Benchmark Date: June 1972

	One Preceding Quarter		One Succeeding Quarter	
	Appreciating Currencies	*Depreciating Currencies*	*Appreciating Currencies*	*Depreciating Currencies*
Cash				
Average level of account	$2,308,000	$7,898,000	$2,795,000	$9,282,000
Average value of positive changes/currency	49%	24%	60%	15%

Table 5A-3 continued

	One Preceding Quarter		One Succeeding Quarter	
	Appreciating Currencies	*Depreciating Currencies*	*Appreciating Currencies*	*Depreciating Currencies*
Average value of negative changes/currency	8%	5%	8%	9%
Forward Contracts				
Average level of account	$4,447,000	$47,000	$4,683,000	−$1,842,000
Average value of positive changes/currency	19%	8%	332%	30%
Average value of negative changes/currency	7%	7%	−	77%
Accounts Receivable				
Average level of account	$5,234,000	$16,363,000	$5,003,000	$16,186,000
Average value of positive changes/currency	11%	6%	4%	12%
Average value of negative changes/currency	8%	5%	10%	3%
Inventory				
Average level of account	$7,243,000	$21,842,000	$7,284,000	$21,014,000
Average value of positive changes/currency	16%	5%	7%	4%
Average value of negative changes/currency	2%	2%	2%	4%
Accounts Payable				
Average level of account	$6,792,000	$26,083,000	$6,703,000	$27,698,000
Average value of positive changes/currency	6%	12%	27%	5%
Average value of negative changes/currency	5%	3%	6%	3%
Short-Term Debt				
Average level of account	$7,051,000	$16,426,000	$6,424,000	$17,314,000
Average value of positive changes/currency	20%	31%	71%	13%
Average value of negative changes/currency	6%	9%	8%	8%
Long-Term Debt				
Average level of account	$9,693,000	$16,617,000	$8,865,000	$17,215,000
Average value of positive changes/currency	18%	3%	4%	3%
Average value of negative changes/currency	4%	4%	3%	3%
Company Definition of Exposure				
Average level of account	−$3,354,000	$3,498,000	−$2,334,000	$1,966,000
Average value of positive changes/currency	43%	15%	16%	11%
Average value of negative changes/currency	10%	9%	15%	29%

Note: Appreciating or strong currencies: Belgian franc, French franc, German mark, guilder, Swiss franc, and yen.

Depreciating or weak currencies: U.S. dollar, Canadian dollar, lira, and pound.

Table 5A-4
Average Levels and Average Percentage Changes in Accounts in Appreciating versus Depreciating Currencies; Benchmark Date: March 1973

	One Preceding Quarter		One Succeeding Quarter	
	Appreciating Currencies	Depreciating Currencies	Appreciating Currencies	Depreciating Currencies
Cash				
Average level of account	$3,022,000	$1,418,000	$2,808,000	$1,024,000
Average value of positive changes/currency	59%	19%	72%	46%
Average value of negative changes/currency	15%	43%	14%	13%
Forward Contracts				
Average level of account	$20,951,000	−$6,511,000	$17,459,000	−$7,357,000
Average value of positive changes/currency	3%	13%	11%	75%
Average value of negative changes/currency	−	597%	3%	200%
Accounts Receivable				
Average level of account	$6,254,000	$7,114,000	$6,496,000	$7,446,000
Average value of positive changes/currency	10%	6%	62%	6%
Average value of negative changes/currency	12%	5%	3%	5%
Inventory				
Average level of account	$8,264,000	$10,676,000	$8,685,000	$11,069,000
Average value of positive changes/currency	7%	4%	4%	5%
Average value of negative changes/currency	3%	3%	3%	3%
Accounts Payable				
Average level of account	$9,026,000	$16,636,000	$9,993,000	$17,290,000
Average value of positive changes/currency	3%	10%	9%	19%
Average value of negative changes/currency	7%	7%	4%	3%
Short-Term Debt				
Average level of account	$8,920,000	$9,337,000	$10,860,000	$5,993,000
Average value of positive changes/currency	46%	17%	13%	5%
Average value of negative changes/currency	5%	3%	3%	6%
Long-Term Debt				
Average level of account	$12,303,000	$10,181,000	$11,394,000	$8,092,000
Average value of positive changes/currency	4%	2%	15%	32%
Average value of negative changes/currency	4%	3%	4%	2%

Table 5A-4 Continued

	One Preceding Quarter		One Succeeding Quarter	
	Appreciating Currencies	*Depreciating Currencies*	*Appreciating Currencies*	*Depreciating Currencies*
Company Definition of Exposure				
Average level of account	−$1,629,000	−$2,626,000	$1,794,000	−$1,964,000
Average value of positive changes/currency	30%	35%	58%	37%
Average value of negative changes/currency	33%	32%	13%	12%

Note: Appreciating or strong currencies: Belgian franc, French franc, German mark, guilder, Swiss franc, and yen.
Depreciating or weak currencies: U.S. dollar, Canadian dollar, lira, and pound.

Table 5A-5
Average Levels and Average Percentage Changes in Accounts in Appreciating versus Depreciating Currencies; Benchmark Date: June 1973

	One Preceding Quarter		One Succeeding Quarter	
	Appreciating Currencies	*Depreciating Currencies*	*Appreciating Currencies*	*Depreciating Currencies*
Cash				
Average level of account	$2,969,000	$1,051,000	$2,717,000	$1,177,000
Average value of positive changes/currency	59%	37%	195%	23%
Average value of negative changes/currency	12%	13%	12%	41%
Forward Contracts				
Average level of account	$17,983,000	−$2,877,000	$14,279,000	$2,056,000
Average value of positive changes/currency	11%	75%	17%	13%
Average value of negative changes/currency	3%	217%	7%	3%
Accounts Receivable				
Average level of account	$7,064,000	$8,829,000	$7,158,000	$9,447,000
Average value of positive changes/currency	62%	4%	15%	236%
Average value of negative changes/currency	3%	5%	4%	3%
Inventory				
Average level of account	$9,327,000	$11,202,000	$9,266,000	$11,744,000
Average value of positive changes/currency	3%	5%	4%	5%
Average value of negative changes/currency	3%	2%	2%	2%

Table 5A-5 Continued

	One Preceding Quarter		One Succeeding Quarter	
	Appreciating Currencies	Depreciating Currencies	Appreciating Currencies	Depreciating Currencies
Accounts Payable				
Average level of account	$10,187,000	$11,484,000	$10,139,000	$10,701,000
Average value of positive changes/currency	10%	16%	5%	8%
Average value of negative changes/currency	6%	9%	6%	10%
Short-Term Debt				
Average level of account	$11,045,000	$5,993,000	$10,591,000	$6,610,000
Average value of positive changes/currency	13%	5%	9%	26%
Average value of negative changes/currency	3%	6%	2%	7%
Long-Term Debt				
Average level of account	$13,214,000	$10,461,000	$13,373,000	$12,062,000
Average value of positive changes/currency	20%	32%	19%	6%
Average value of negative changes/currency	4%	2%	3%	6%
Company Definition of Exposure				
Average level of account	−$2,259,000	−$389	−$1,872	$1,021
Average value of positive changes/currency	60%	38%	14%	10%
Average value of negative changes/currency	13%	20%	31%	16%

Note: Appreciating or strong currencies: Belgian franc, French franc, German mark, guilder, Swiss franc, and yen.

Depreciating weak currencies: U.S. dollar, Canadian dollar, lira, and pound.

6 Summary and Implications

The objective of the study reported in this book was to obtain a better understanding of the process involved in the foreign-exchange management decision and its bearing on foreign-exchange market fluctuations. So, I asked the managers how they made their decisions and requested figures showing how managers' earlier decisions had been reached. The managers provided very specific information on the various parts of the foreign-exchange management decision, including some sample decisions. The historical figures served to permit a cross-examination of the statements made by the managers and to allow an objective evaluation of the relationship between these managers' decisions and the turmoils in the exchange markets.

The managers interviewed were financial officers of seventy U.S. multinationals. The companies were selected from among the Fortune 500 for their heavy involvement in Europe and Japan—the countries whose currencies were of most interest in this study. The quantitative data were obtained from thirty-six of the companies interviewed. They represented accounts in each currency for each of the major subsidiaries located in Europe and Japan. The period intended to be covered was 1967 to 1974; however, data were not available for the earlier years in many of the companies.

The Managerial Process

The Objective

Essentially, the managers interviewed perceived their job in the area of foreign-exchange management as *protecting* their companies from the fluctuations in exchange rates. The emphasis was definitely on a defensive position. Trying to *profit* from the movements in the exchange markets was not considered an objective by any of the managers interviewed. The often-heard statement "We do not speculate" voices this position well. These managers considered the profit-making objective to be one appropriate for exchange traders, not for nonfinancial corporations.

It could be argued that the difference between the objective of protecting and profiting from movements in the exchange markets is only one of degree, but these managers were very insistent in maintaining the distinction. Perhaps because of the stigma attached to the word *speculation*, which presumes it is destabilizing, and the associated fear of government intervention to prevent destabilizing speculation, these managers wished to disassociate themselves totally from anything that could be construed as speculative behavior in their exchange management conduct. Later in this chapter, I will question the implications of this wish to stay away from so-called speculative behavior for the stability of the exchange market.

To protect the company against the effects of exchange fluctuations requires a knowledge of the exposure of the company to exchange risk. This exposure can be measured in multiple ways. It can be measured according to certain accounting conventions or in terms of cash flow changes. It can be measured by using historical figures or projecting the figures into the future. The two best known exposure measures are translation exposure, which is computed according to certain accounting conventions, and transaction exposure, which is computed in terms of cash flows involving conversions in the exchange markets. Either one can be calculated using historical figures or projected ones.

The exposure measure most commonly used by the managers interviewed was translation exposure computed for the current reporting period. During the 1974 interviews, translation exposure was used almost exclusively in these companies. However, by 1977 transaction exposure was followed simultaneously in most of the companies. Although Statement No. 8 of the Financial Accounting Standards Board (FASB #8), imposing a single method for computing translation exposure, became effective in January 1976, in 1977 translation exposure appeared to have a reduced role compared to earlier years when it was the only measure used. In spite of the very strong criticism of FASB #8 from managers (or maybe because of this criticism), only 20 percent of the companies interviewed in 1977 based their hedging decisions solely on translation exposure. The other companies used transaction exposure, a modified FASB #8 measure, or a combination of the three measures when contemplating hedging policies.

The dichotomy between translation and transaction exposure is reminiscent of the old controversy in financial theory of whether earnings per share or cash flow maximization should be the objective of the financial manager. The effects of exchange fluctuations on translation exposure appear as exchange gains or losses in the income statement. Translation exposure affects earnings per share directly. The effects of exchange fluctuations on the company's future exchange conversions, that is, transaction exposure, may not even appear on the period's financial reports at all and therefore have no impact on current earnings per share. Of course, eventually these cash flows will be reflected on future financial statements. But for the manager concerned with current reported earnings per share, this fact about the future is only of secondary importance—by that time he or she may have moved on to be president of the company!

The increased emphasis on transaction exposure between 1974 and 1977 also parallels the development among practitioners who historically have placed increasing weight on forecast cash flows, in contrast to reported earnings, in more recent years. However, the interest in transaction exposure falls short of an interest in *all* the company's cash flows. Transaction exposure refers to specific cash flows involving exchange transactions. If a company's cash flow does not involve an exchange transaction during the relevant time period, it is not part of transaction exposure. In the very long run, by the time the foreign subsidiary is liquidated, most cash flows involving a single currency will have been reflected eventually in an exchange transaction, and therefore in transaction exposure. However, because of the short horizon within which transaction exposure is measured (usually a year or less), most of these other cash flows are never included in the definition of transaction exposure.

Responsibility for Control of Exposure

When asked who is responsible for managing exposure to exchange risk in this company, the managers always answered with the name of a unit or person who invariably worked for the treasury or finance department. The exposure to which these managers referred was the consolidated exposure for the company as a whole. This exposure was computed for specific dates from reports submitted by individual foreign units—either specialized exposure reports or regular financial reports. But at this point, the responsibility for managing the exchange risk appeared to concentrate solely in the treasury department. Exposure management seemed to be highly centralized in these companies. However, this may have been so only when a narrow definition of exposure management was used.

We can think of exposure to exchange risk from two different angles. In a dynamic sense, a whole range of separate business decisions do have exchange exposure implications. These are the typical business decisions which marketing, production, finance, and all the other areas make in their normal operations. Many of these decisions do have implications for exposure to exchange risk of the company. In a static sense, we have the exposure to exchange risk computed at any given time. This exposure incorporates portions of earlier business decisions, and depending on the time horizon of the exposure figure, it may incorporate the result of business decisions to be made in the future.

It is this last type of exposure, the one computed after the fact, that these managers had in mind when suggesting a high degree of centralization in exposure management. This ex post figure, indeed, usually was the responsibility of the treasury department. But the fact is that exposures to exchange risk are generated and acted on throughout the whole business. When we incorporate this dimension in the definition of exposure management, it does not appear so centralized and several conflicts do come up.

Decisions in business can be grouped into two major types: operations (marketing, production, and so on) and finance. For simplicity's sake, let's say that these decisions can be made only by foreign operating units or the treasury department. Since both types of decisions can have implications for the company's exposure to exchange risk, the distribution of the control and responsibility for these decisions around the company determines who actually manages the exposure to exchange risk in the company.

Operating decisions are universally controlled by operating management who, by and large, are also held accountable for the exchange implications of these decisions. Very few foreign units were evaluated solely in terms of operating profits denominated in local currency; in most cases the evaluation of operating performance was in dollars. Financing decisions, on the other hand, are sometimes controlled by the operating units and at other times controlled by the treasury department. The operating units are sometimes held accountable for the exchange implications of these financing decisions, and at other times they are not, and control and responsibility are not necessarily matched. In some companies the foreign units did not control the financing decisions but were still held accountable for profits after financing charges. So, indeed, the control and responsibility for exposure to exchange risk are distributed throughout the company.

Then, as a top layer to the above, we have the treasury department which is told it is responsible for managing the exposure of the company to exchange risk. When exchange gains and losses appear in the financial statements, the treasury department is usually held responsible.

Let us consider some of the implications of this dissemination of exposure management throughout the company.

Excluding the treasury department from many of the operating decisions has made it possible for important exposures to go unnoticed until they were formalized in some financial report, long after the decision related to the exposure had been made. Commitments are often made without consulting financial officers, who then discover an exposure only when something such as a payable in a foreign currency appears among the accounts to be settled for the month. A typical example of this state of affairs is the company which embarked on the production of a new product using a major component produced in Germany. Production management and marketing personnel worked closely to design and measure the potential of this product and to determine whether it was best to manufacture or to buy this important component. Treasury did know of the development and even participated in calculating the profitability of the product. However, treasury was totally excluded from the negotiations with the German manufacturer. It was only after the fact, when the production managers in the United States began complaining about the increasing cost of this component—the contract price had been negotiated in marks—that the financial officer in charge of managing the exposure to exchange risk for the company was informed of the situation and asked to do something about it. Not many options were left at this point.

Most practitioners would agree that it is appropriate that financial officers should not feel free to interfere with operations. However, if exposure to exchange risk is to be the responsibility of treasury, the finance department must have information as exposures develop throughout the company. Production and management personnel have a tendency to consider financial matters outside their scope and therefore destined to be ignored. These managers often consider exchange exposure just another financial problem, which it is. But operating decisions do have exchange exposure implications, and unless treasury knows about them on time, alternative options may go unnoticed until it is too late. In general, a greater awareness of the problem would help improve the situation in many companies.

Among financing decisions, one particular arrangement has the potential for producing conflicts similar to the ones just described. This is the case when the subsidiary controls its own financing and is also held accountable for it, while the treasury department remains in charge of the exposure to exchange risk for the company as a whole. This could possibly leave treasury outside the negotiations for financing and therefore unaware of exposures. However, operating units, when given the flexibility to arrange for their own financing, generally choose their local currency. If that source of funds is considered too expensive, then the company's treasury department becomes involved in helping to find an alternative source. Either way, the treasury is informed of the exposure implications of financing arranged by the operating units.

At the other extreme is the arrangement where the treasury department controls all the financing of foreign units. The conflicts in this case are of a different nature. They occur when the foreign units are held accountable for the exchange implications of these decisions, for example, when they are evaluated in terms of profits after financing, in either dollars or local currency. Here the treasury department is in charge of something it fully controls, but internally the foreign units are asked to accept the implications of decisions they did not make. Although the management of exposure to exchange risk is helped by the centralization of financing decisions, internal conflicts can make this centralization very expensive. In addition, excluding the operating units from the financing decisions can have an effect similar to the one when the treasury was excluded from operating decisions. Information about local financial markets may be missed by the treasury department because the operating units are not asked to search for it in order to particpate in the decision.

By concentrating on the management of exposures after they have developed, the treasury department can pretend to run a highly centralized system of exposure management. However, this is only part of the picture. An important dimension of exposure to exchange risk is being ignored or managed in haphazard fashion. Exchange fluctuations affect the value of operating cash flows, and decisions which affect operating cash flows affect the company's exposure to exchange risk. The exposure-management systems in existence in most companies practically ignore this basic fact. Not only is treasury not asked to participate in operating decisions which have important exposure implications, but treasury itself chose to define exposure in terms which exclude the impact of exchange fluctuations on operating cash flows. As pointed out at the end of the preceding section, there has been increased attention to the exposure involved on cash flows involving exchange transactions, in contrast to translation exposure. However, this interest in cash flows is still far from being extended to operating cash flows in general, regardless of whether they involve exchange transactions in the near future.

It is true that production knows best about widgets and treasury knows best about money. However, unless production knows more about the implications of alternative decisions for the company's exposure, and treasury knows more about the implications of its financing decisions for the local manager's performance, less than optimal decisions will be made by both.

Modification of the exposure reporting systems in use now could go a long way to accomplish a better coordination between operating decisions and exposure management. Current reporting systems concentrate on translation and transaction exposure with a maximum horizon of usually a year. That is, they require a report of the balance sheet accounts in different currencies and a report of cash flows requiring conversions in the exchange markets within the near future. A list of commitments not yet in the books is part of the reporting system of a few companies, and in most the treasury department does not consider it a reliable listing. Surprise payments and receipts occur all the time. In any case, these commitments refer to only a portion of the cash flows—those involving exchange transactions within a relatively short period of time. Operating cash flows not requiring exchange conversions in the near future were ignored for the most part.

The only attempt to measure the impact of exchange fluctuations on the value of operating cash flows was done only indirectly, by using a modification to translation exposure. This was the case for the companies who considered their economic exposure as FASB #8 plus inventory. The presumption was that no price change could take place for at least one turnover period, so when a devaluation took place, it would affect fully the sales for that period. The concern of these officers with devaluations of foreign currencies and the inability to increase local prices because of price controls is behind this measure. In the more recent world where the devaluing currency has been the dollar and not the foreign currency, the comparable presumption would have been that for one turnover period prices could not be *reduced* to compensate for the upvaluation of the foreign currency. In this context, the earlier reasoning sounds absurd.

What the reporting system must include is an evaluation of how exchange fluctuations in either direction would affect revenues and costs whether requiring exchange transactions or not. This would accomplish two things. It would force operating personnel to focus on the problem and hopefully include exchange considerations in their decisions, and it would alert the treasury department to the exchange implications of decisions made by operating management. A better dialogue between operating units and treasury in the area of exposure to exchange risk may be one of the byproducts.

The Personal Element

Earlier in this chapter we pointed out that the concern of the managers interviewed with translation exposure paralleled their concern with reported earnings per share. However, these managers' concern with reported financial statements went one step further (or nearer) than earnings per share. These managers focused on the effects of exchange fluctuations on one special account in the income statement—foreign-exchange gains and losses. Even when other accounts, such as interest expense, may have been affected simultaneously, these managers were particularly preoccupied with the effects of exchange fluctuations on the foreign-exchange account. This was in spite of the fact that it is the combination of the exchange account and the other accounts affected by exchange fluctuations which determines the bottom line in the income statement. The special visibility of the exchange gains and losses account appears to have prompted many of these managers to follow a different (ir)rationale from the economist's maximization principle.

The managers' special behavior was observed in two areas: their selection of hedging tools and their sample hedging decisions.

Among the tools available to cover exposures, leading and lagging payments together with direct money market transfers were the preferred instruments to modify unwanted exposures. Forward-exchange contracts often were referred to as a measure of last resort. That is, tools involving borrowing and investing in different currencies were preferred to the forward-exchange market. Given the close relationship between interest differentials and forward rates, this preference requires additional explanation.

One rationale for preferring money market instruments over forward-exchange contracts involves the differences in reporting interest income and expenses from reporting exchange gains and losses. Interest income and expense associated with hedging an exposure in the money market are reported with all the other income and expense of the company. Gains and losses in forward contracts are reported with foreign-exchange gains and losses—a distinct account. Managers' aversion to reporting anything called exchange losses may have deterred the use of forward-exchange contracts in many cases.

Of course, there is another less rational explanation for the reluctance to use forward-exchange contracts. This is the lack of familiarity with the foreign-exchange market relative to the better understanding of the traditional financing techniques of borrowing and investing. This attitude is consistent with the practice of companies where forward-exchange contracts are given very special attention. An example of such treatment is the company where the assistant treasurer had permission to borrow up to $250,000 without needing further approval within the company. However, he had to ask permission from the president of the company for engaging in any forward-exchange contract in excess of $10,000. The special significance attached to forward-exchange contracts is clear in the cases of several of the managers who stated that they did not use forward-exchange contracts because it was not their practice to speculate in the foreign-exchange market!

The managers' special preferences were also evident in their responses to the question of whether they would hedge a given exposure. These managers were asked to assume conditions in the market which represented an efficient market. They were told that the forward rate was the best forecast available of the future spot rate. That is, the rate for covering the exposure, the forward rate, was the same as the future spot rate anticipated by the market. The comparison of the rate locked in by the hedging operation and the spot rate expected to prevail in the future should have left these managers indifferent as to whether to hedge the given exposures.

In fact, the interviews reported in this book showed that management was far from being indifferent about the exchange-management decision. Either management did not believe the forward rate anticipated the future spot rate, or management based its decisions at least partially on something other than average expected values. This "something" appeared to be the sign of the expected outcome. Whether on average an exchange gain or an exchange loss was expected was a major factor in these managers' hedging decisions.

When an exchange loss was expected and the forward rate was selling at a discount, the majority of these managers preferred to hedge the exposure rather than to leave it open. When an exchange gain was expected and the forward rate was selling at a premium, only a minority of these managers chose to hedge the exposure. Because of the assumed conditions, the loss locked in by the forward contract in the first case equaled the expected loss if the positions were left open; and the exchange gain expected in the second case when the positions were left open equaled the premium that could be obtained if the exposure were covered.

Management does not appear to analyze the hedging decision in terms of the average expected gain or loss. Instead, management shows a particular aversion to reporting exchange losses. If the average expectation is for an exchange loss, management is eager to see that a loss larger than the average expected, the forward rate, is not realized. On the other hand, if the average expected represents an exchange gain, management is more willing to be exposed to the vagaries of the market.

In the assumed conditions these managers did not have to pay any price to satisfy their risk preferences. On average, the expected value of the exposure was the same whether covered or not. However, it is easy to extrapolate the behavior observed and to conclude that these managers' risk aversion would make them willing to pay a premium to avoid reporting exchange losses. They would be willing to hedge a positive exposure at a forward rate which is below the expected depreciation in the spot rate. The additional cost of the forward cover would be considered worth paying to avoid the eventuality of reporting an exchange loss if the exposure were left uncovered and the spot rate depreciated more than the average amount expected. On the other hand, the premium on the forward rate would have to be substantially above the expected exchange appreciation before these managers would be induced to hedge a positive exposure. Once the possibilities of reporting exchange losses have been reduced to an acceptable level—very low in case of a positive exposure in an appreciating currency—these managers would rather not lock in an exchange gain. Instead they prefer to be exposed to a potentially larger or smaller exchange gain, but a gain.

When we analyzed in chapter 4 the quantitative data obtained from the exposure reports of these companies, the results also indicated a reluctance of these managers to report exchange losses. One dollar of expected exchange losses is not neutralized by one dollar of expected exchange gains in these managers' minds. After the financing accounts—cash and debt—were segregated from the other accounts, certain patterns emerged. These financial accounts, over which the finance department can be presumed to have more control, tended to counteract the exposures generated by operations when this exposure was likely to generate exchange losses. This was particularly clear in the case of the pound, where financial accounts tended to reduce the positive exposures generated by the operating accounts, and in the Swiss franc, where the financing accounts tended to counteract a very large negative exposure existing at the beginning of the period because of large borrowings in this currency. In the currencies which tended to appreciate during the period the financing accounts did not show any specific pattern. However, the movement of the financial variables still left the majority of the exposures in these currencies on the positive side.

MNCs and Exchange-Market Stability

The Issues

Multinational companies have been accused of being a major force behind the exchange crises of the 1970s. The presumption is that MNC behavior has contributed to increase the magnitude of the crises, if not to initiate them. They have been accused of speculating in the exchange markets. However, whether they did speculate does not prove their role in the exchange crises one way or the other.

Speculation is a word with a very high emotional charge. On one extreme, liberal economists have enshrined speculators as the guarantors of the workings of the free-market economy. But speculators have also been accused, usually by government officials, of bringing about the collapse of otherwise stable markets. Whether speculators perform a useful function depends on whether their speculations tend to stabilize or destabilize the markets. Liberal economists, who endorse the system of freely floating exchange rates, believe that speculators stabilize the markets. Government officials who find themselves at their wits' ends in trying to stabilize the markets often believe that the source of their pains and tribulations is the destabilizing behavior of speculators.

The reason destabilizing speculation is loathed by everybody is that it produces a "wrong" exchange rate, one which does not represent the "true" underlying economic conditions, whatever they may be. This departure from the "true" rate has costs to society in general and to practitioners in particular. The instability created by the wrong rates increases the risk of international business. When an importer purchases foreign goods denominated in a foreign currency, she or he does not know what the final price in terms of her or his currency will be. This increases the difficulties of doing business internationally for the people involved. It may deter international trade, and this has poor implications for the economies involved in general.

As the so-called wrong rate continues to prevail through time, other prices in the economy also start becoming "wrong." Let's say that the dollar depreciates more than what the economic conditions warrant. The undervalued currency makes the exports from the United States more attractive. This increases employment in the export industries and decreases it in other industries. This has costs in retraining labor and expanding capacity in the export sector. However, these costs are not so bad compared to what happens when the cycle is reversed. When the cycle reverses, all these unnecessary adjustments also have to be reversed. This time it will be more painful because it will increase unemployment. All these unnecessary shifts in resources have very high social and political costs.

The dislocations created by the instability just described explain the concern about speculators who may be the source of such instability. It also explains how the policy implication of such analysis in many circles is that speculators should be controlled. The accusation that the MNCs were speculating in the exchange markets actually is an accusation that they were engaging in destabilizing speculation. Most neutral observers would not object to MNCs or any other market participant engaging in stabilizing speculation.

So, the question as to the role of MNCs in the exchange markets can be rephrased in terms of whether they were engaging in speculative activities which would have proved destabilizing to the exchange markets. We can also ask whether the MNCs engage in general activites, speculative or not, which may contribute to the instability of the exchange markets. Before we do this, let's define what stabilizing and destabilizing speculation involves.

We can think of a series of exchange rates which would exist in the absence of speculators. These exchange rates would be determined by the underlying economic forces. For example, as the exports of a nation increased relative to its imports, we would expect its exchange rate to appreciate relative to the other currencies. When exports decreased later on, its exchange rate would depreciate then from its appreciated value. Enter the speculator. If the speculator saw that the increase in exports was due simply to a cyclical phenomenon to be reversed after a few months, he or she will also see that the appreciation in the currency's exchange rate was to be reversed in the near future. To profit from this analysis, the speculator will sell its inventory of the currency as the exchange rate started to appreciate and buy it when the rate started to depreciate. These two actions, being contrary to the exchange-rate movements which the fluctuations in exports produced, would tend to reduce the amplitude of that fluctuation. That is, in this case the actions of the speculator helped stabilize the exchange markets. Because of the speculator the exchange rate fluctuated less than it would have fluctuated in the absence of him or her.

Let us say now that the speculator who saw the exchange rate appreciate in response to the increased exports decided that this was only the beginning of a very long trend not to be reversed in the near future. He or she could have reached such a conclusion either because of a poor reading of the economic situation or because he or she expected the market to think so—even though the speculator knew better. Now, as the exchange rate began to appreciate, the speculator buys increasing amounts of the currency, and does not sell as in the previous case. This buying of the currency on top of the appreciating moves generated by the exports will produce an appreciation of that currency larger than it would have been in the absence of the speculator. Similar reasoning could be used to explain how the speculator would increase the amount a currency depreciates. If the speculator does not expect the sources of the depreciation to reverse themselves in the near future, the speculator will sell that currency, thus contributing further to its decrease in value.

Stabilizing speculation involves buying the currency when it is cheap and selling it when it is dear. This reduces the amplitude of the fluctuations of what the market prices would have been in the absence of the speculator. Destabilizing speculators continue buying and selling the currency long past the point where the exchange rate based on basic economic forces should be.

The problem with this definition of stabilizing and destabilizing speculation is that it requires a knowledge of the equilibrium exchange rate dictated by underlying economic conditions. That rate, unfortunately, is never quoted in the market. Consensus as to what it should be is rarely reached by either economists or politicians from different nations.

Empirically we have to study the behavior of MNCs independently of the path of equilibrium exchange rate. We have to ask whether there is anything in the behavior of MNCs which would tend to magnify the amplitude of the market swings.

The Evidence

In the absence of a knowledge of what the true exchange rate should be, we can analyze the requirements for speculation to be stabilizing and then see whether the behavior of MNCs conforms to these requirements. Stabilizing speculation involves the following: (1) good forecasting ability so that the speculators can sell when the exchange rate is overvalued and buy when it is undervalued; (2) willingness to move funds from one currency to another in response to changes in *expected* yields.

Chapter 5 showed that around periods marked as exchange crises the MNCs tended to hold larger amounts of liquid funds in the so-called strong currencies than in weaker currencies. As operations generated funds in weak currencies, often they were converted to other currencies. But when during these periods of crises operations generated funds in the strong currencies, the MNCs often were reluctant to convert those funds into other currencies. Although there is no evidence that these companies increased their borrowings in weak currencies, presumably to transfer them into stronger ones, the management of internally generated funds had a similar effect. It increased the supply of depreciating currencies and decreased the supply of appreciating currencies. This is similar to selling the depreciating currency and buying the appreciating one.

The management of internally generated funds in these companies during exchange crises was consistent with good forecasting ability.[1] These companies certainly helped to bring about the depreciations and appreciations of the currencies involved. Now, this does not prove that their transfers of funds were necessarily stabilizing. If they helped to accelerate the exchange rate moves which were dictated anyhow by economic conditions, these companies helped to stabilize the exchange markets. But if the flow of funds created by these companies just served to create a bandwagon effect where appreciations and depreciations were much bigger than justified by general economic conditions, then their funds management proved destabilizing to the market. However, as mentioned before, we cannot judge these companies by making reference to a "true" exchange rate. That is not observable.

The exposure data analyzed in chapter 4 showed some evidence that the transfer of funds generated internally during crisis periods was also characteristic for the whole period from 1967 to 1974. In that chapter we took into account some of the imperfections which characterized the markets during the period. In particular, we examined the relationship which these companies' transfer of funds may have had with the nature of exchange controls which prevailed throughout the period. However, as shown in chapter 2, we also have some evidence on how these managers reached hedging decisions under market conditions consistent with an efficient market. Although exchange controls would have facilitated the described pattern of transfer of funds, the managers reached similar decisions when the assumed conditions did not involve any market imperfection. Another factor seems to be a better explanation: the managers' particular risk aversion.[2]

The research presented in this book supports the argument that these managers do not perceive themselves as engaging in speculation, but rather as protecting the value of their companies' foreign assets. If for speculators the sequence of events is one where they look at expected rates and then decide what position to take in different currencies, for these managers the sequence is reversed. These managers look at the positions which their companies' operations present them and then look at expected rates to decide whether to keep them or hedge them. However, in making this decision, they go further than just comparing expected values. To them, one dollar of expected exchange gains is not enough to compensate for one dollar of expected exchange losses. They do not base their decisions on expected values, independently of the risks involved. That is, they are not risk-neutral. In particular, they are very reluctant to report exchange losses.

The particular risk preferences of these managers made them transfer funds whenever the company's position would have generated exchange losses and not do much when the company's position would entail exchange gains. Given that profitable operations generate funds internally, this means that these companies' positions tended to generate exchange losses in depreciating currencies and exchange gains in appreciating currencies. Therefore, the observed tendency to move funds away from depreciating currencies and leave them in appreciating currencies.

The effect of this behavior on the market is as follows: In depreciating currencies, the companies sold the currencies. They did not want to hold a positive position in these currencies. Even in cases where a reversal of the exchange rate might have been foreseen, the concern with current reported exchange losses would have made these managers sell the currency. For appreciating currencies, the opposite was true. Basically, these companies were not willing to move funds from one currency to another in response to changes in expected yields. They could not have acted as a stabilizing influence. And their particular risk preferences tended to increase the instability in the market.

In the interviews these managers were given conditions where they should have been indifferent between hedging or not hedging their positions. Still they hedged the positive positions in depreciating currencies more often than the positive exposures in appreciating currencies. Empirically we do not know what these managers thought the expected cost of hedging was relative to the cost of maintaining the positions. However, their aversion to reporting exchange losses could easily be transferred to a willingness to pay a higher hedging cost than the average exchange depreciation anticipated. In this case, even if the rest of the market flows were stabilizing, thus producing a forward-exchange rate which reflected the future spot rate consistent with underlying economic conditions, the willingness of these companies to continue selling the currency would bring that rate past what the market would have done otherwise. The additional decline of the currency, which the MNCs would have been willing to pay for when reflected in the forward rate, would have been the responsibility of these companies. In these cases it could be said they had contributed to destabilize the exchange market.

During the period studied these companies moved funds in sympathy with the tides in the exchange markets. This by itself does not prove or disprove that their actions were destabilizing. However, the financial officers' risk aversion clearly is a factor which has the potential to increase the instability in the market. Probably, the larger the expected change, the larger the contribution of instability, as the MNCs' stakes on exchange losses become larger.

However, these managers were *not* trying to destabilize the exchange market on purpose, but were responding to the demands of their environment. In the words of one of these managers, "If I generate exchange gains, I am just doing my job; however, if exchange losses have to be reported, the roof falls in." Limiting the size of reported exchange losses in this environment is a rational decision, even if a premium must be paid at times.

Notes

1. A study of the exchange positions of U.S. banks and nonbanks compiled by the U.S. Treasury Department for the period March 1975 to March 1978 suggests that U.S. firms are not very good at forecasting foreign-exchange rates. On this ground the activites of these companies are doubted to be stabilizing to the exchange market. See Normal S. Fieleke, "Foreign-Exchange Speculation by U.S. Firms: Some New Evidence," *New England Economic Review*, March-April 1979, pp. 5-17.

2. For an analysis of the effect of exchange-risk preferences on the stability of exchange rates, see Jacques R. Artus and Andrew D. Crockett, *Floating Exchange Rates and the Need for Surveillance*, Essays in International Finance No. 127, International Finance Section, Princeton University, Princeton, N.J., May 1978, and Clas Wihlborg, *Currency Risks in International Financial Markets*, Princeton Studies in International Finance No. 44, Princeton University, Princeton, N.J., December 1978.

Appendix A
List of Companies
in Sample

*Abbott Laboratories
*American Can Company
*AMF, Inc.
American Metal Climax, Inc.
American Smelting and Refining Co.
Becton, Dickinson and Company
*Bendix International
*Borden, Inc.
Bristol—Myers Company
Brunswick Corporation
*Burroughs Corporation
*The Carborundum Company
*Chrysler Corporation
*Continental Oil Company
CPC International
*Continental Can Company
Deere and Company
*Dow Chemical
E.I. duPont de Nemours and
Co., Inc.
Eastman Kodak Company
Eaton Corporation
*Eli Lilly and Company
*Esmark, Inc.
*Exxon Corporation
FMC Corporation
Ford Motor Company
*General Electric Company
General Foods Corporation
*General Mills, Inc.
General Motors Corporation
*The Gillette Company
GTE International
Gulf Oil Company
Hercules, Inc.
*Honeywell, Inc.

*IBM Corporation
*I.C. Industries
*Inmont Corporation
*International Harvester Company
*International Paper Company
International Telephone &
Telegraph Co.
Ingersoll-Rand Company
*Johns-Manville Corporation
Kraftco Corporation
Libby, McNeill & Libby
Maremont Corporation
*Merck and Company
Mobil Oil Corporation
*Nabisco, Inc.
*National Cash Register Company
*Norton Company
Pepsico, Inc.
Pfizer, Inc.
Phillips Petroleum Company
*Polaroid Corporation
*Quaker Oats Company
*Ralston Purina Company
Raytheon Corporation
Reynolds Aluminum
Richardson-Merrell, Inc.
*Scott Paper
*The Singer Company
Sperry Rand Corporation
Squibb Corporation
*Time, Inc.
*Uniroyal, Inc.
USM Corporation
*W.R. Grace and Company
Westinghouse Electric Corp.
Xerox Corporation

*Companies providing quantitative data.

Appendix B
Questionnaire
Administered in 1974

(Numbers on the left are the percentage of the companies responding to the question who chose the specific answer. For a discussion of how this interview was administered see the introductory section to chapter 2.)

Total Size: _____ million sales   Company _____

International Size: _____ million sales   Manager _____

          Date _____

I. *Introduction*
   1. How is international business organized?
      49 International division reporting to top executive
      24 By products, combined with U.S. operations
       3 By functional areas, say, finance, production, and so on
      24 Mixed system

   2. Foreign ownership policy
      13 Only sole ownership
       8 Only joint ventures
      47 Sole ownership except where impossible
      32 Not a predetermined policy, depends on the case

   3. Degree of intercompany trade
      75 Significant
      25 Insignificant

   4. Currency of intercompany trade
      31 U.S. dollars
      40 Currency of producer
      24 Depends on tax and foreign-exchange considerations
       5 Other

   5. Degree of exports to third parties from the United States
      50 Significant
      50 Insignificant

   6. Currency of exports to third parties from the United States
      86 U.S. dollars
       7 Depends on market conditions
       7 Depends on foreign-exchange considerations

7. Responsibility for raising short-term funds
   36 Almost totally centralized at headquarters
   58 Subsidiary responsible for raising its own funds
      51 General guidelines given
      _7 General guidelines not given
    _6 Subsidiary responsible for presenting proposal, final decision made by headquarters

II. *System to monitor exposure to foreign-exchange risk*
   1. Accounting definition of exposure:
      Accounts translated at current exchange rates "C"

      Accounts translated at historical exchange rates "H"

   2. What types of foreign-exchange reports do foreign units prepare? (Give sample)
      41 None
      _9 Net by currency
      50 Disaggregated by currency and account

   3. What is the timing of exposure reports?
      54 Historical exposure
      22 Forecast exposure
      24 Both

   4. Are taxes considered in calculating exposure?
      26 Exposure is *after* taxes
      74 Exposure is *before* taxes

III. *Forecast of foreign-exchange rates*
   1. Sources of forecasts (multiple choices are possible)
      38 Buys service
      51 Relies on banks
      27 Relies on foreign subsidiaries
      27 In-house economic department
      31 Miscellaneous

   2. How frequently are foreign-exchange forecasts revised?
      _5 Daily
      _5 Weekly
      _5 Biweekly
      40 Monthly
      20 Quarterly
      25 Unspecified

3. How far into the future are foreign-exchange rates forecast?
    _4_ Only imminent changes
    _4_ A month
    _8_ A quarter
    19   Six months
    77   A year
    _8_ More than a year

4. Methodology for forecasts
    _3_ Formal economic model
    97   Management consensus

IV. *Foreign-exchange management policies*
    1. Assume a large positive exposure in a currency and specified spot and
        forward rates
        a. Foreign-exchange forecast is for large devaluation
            i.   Maximum possible devaluation is larger than possible up-
                 valuation
                 _7_ Will leave position open
                 82   Will bring position to zero
                 11   Will bring position to be negative
            ii. Forecast is subject to high degree of uncertainty
                 40   Will leave position open
                 60   Will bring position to zero
        b. Forecast calls for a stable currency
            82   Will leave position open
            18   Will bring position to zero
        c. Forecast is for an upvaluation. Maximum possible upvaluation is
            larger than possible devaluation
            42   Will leave position open
            13   Will bring it to zero
            29   Will make it even more positive
            16   Will lock in the gain in the forward market

    2. Rank the tools for adjusting exposure according to the use you have
        made of them in the past (tool most used = 1; tool least used = 4)
        1.68 Intercompany accounts (leads and lags)
        1.87 Borrowing plus transfer of funds
        2.49 Forward market
        3.74 Accounts payable and receivable with third parties

Appendix C
Questionnaire
Administered in 1977

(Numbers on the left are the percentage of the companies responding to the question who chose the specific answer. For a discussion of how this interview was administered see the introductory section to chapter 2.)

Company _____

Manager _____

Date _____

I.   What do you consider to be the components of *economic exposure* in your company?

Yes	No	
86	14	FASB #8 definition
59	41	Inventory
8	92	Future profits
41	59	Forecast balance sheet
55	45	Exchange transactions

II. What is the exposure definition used as a target for covering?
     60 Transaction exposure
     20 FASB #8
     20 FASB #8 plus inventory

III. Impact of FASB #8 on your exchange-management operations
     57 No impact
     20 More attention given to foreign-exchange exposure
     20 More inclined to cover exposures
      3 Change financing patterns

IV. Where is responsibility for raising short-term funds located?
     28 Subsidiary
     21 Subsidiary up to a limit
     51 Centralized at headquarters

V.   At what level in the income statement are foreign units evaluated?
     18 Local currency operating profits before interest
     21 Local currency profits after taxes

11 Dollar operating profits before interest and taxes
 9 Dollar profits before taxes but including balance sheet translation
 3 Dollar profits after taxes excluding balance sheet translation
32 Dollar profits after taxes including balance sheet translation
 6 Dollar profits after taxes including and excluding balance sheet translation

Bibliography

International Monetary System

Aliber, Robert Z. "The Interest Rate Parity Theorem: A Reinterpretation." *Journal of Political Economy*, December 1973, pp. 1451-1459.

Balassa, Bela. "The Purchasing-Power Parity Doctrine: A Re-appraisal." *Journal of Policical Economy* 72 (1964):584-596.

Bergsten, C. Fred. *The Dilemmas of the Dollar*. New York: New York University Press for the Council on Foreign Relations, 1975.

Bilson, John F.O. "The Monetary Approach to the Exchange Rate: Some Empirical Evidence." *International Monetary Fund Staff Papers*, March 1978, pp. 48-75.

Brittain, Bruce. "Tests of Theories of Exchange Rate Determination." *Journal of Finance*, May 1977, pp. 519-529.

Burns, Arthur F. "The Need for Order in International Finance." *Columbia Journal of World Business*, Spring 1977, pp. 5-12.

Coombs, Charles A. *The Arena of International Finance*. New York: Wiley-Interscience, 1976.

Corden, W.M. *Inflation, Exchange Rates, and the World Economy: Lectures on International Monetary Economics*. Chicago: University of Chicago Press, 1977.

Day, William H.D. "Flexible Exchange Rates: A Case for Official Intervention." *International Monetary Fund Staff Papers*, July 1977, pp. 330-343.

Frenkel, Jacob A. "The Purchasing Power Parity: Doctrinal Perspective and Evidence from the 1920's." *Journal of International Economics*, May 1978 pp. 169-92.

Frenkel, Jacob A., and Harry G. Johnson, eds. *The Monetary Approach to the Balance of Payments*. Toronto: University of Toronto Press, 1976.

Friedman, Milton, and Robert V. Roosa. "Free versus Fixed Exchange Rates: A Debate." *Journal of Portfolio Management*, Spring 1977, pp. 68-73.

Gailliot, Henry J. "Purchasing Power Parity as an Explanation of Long-Term Changes in Exchange Rates." *Journal of Money, Credit and Banking*, August 1870, pp. 347-357.

International Monetary Fund. *The Monetary Approach to the Balance of Payments: A Collection of Research Papers by Members of the Staff of the International Monetary Fund*. Washington: International Monetary Fund, 1977.

Johnson, Harry G. *The Problem of International Monetary Reform*. London: Athlone Press, 1974.

_____. "The Monetary Approach to the Balance of Payments Theory and Policy: Explanation and Policy Implications." *Economica*, August 1977, pp. 217-229.

_____. "The Monetary Approach to the Balance of Payments: A Nontechnical Guide." *Journal of International Economics*, August 1977, pp. 251-268.

Mussa, Michael. "Our Recent Experience with Fixed and Flexible Exchange Rates: A Comment." In Karl Brunner and Allan Meltzer, eds., *Institutional Arrangements and the Inflation Problem*. Carnegie-Rochester Series on Public Policy, vol. 3. Amsterdam: North Holland, 1976, pp. 123-139.

Officer, Lawrence H. "The Purchasing Power Parity Theory of Exchange Rates: A Review Article." Washington: *International Monetary Fund Staff Papers*, March 1976, pp. 1-60.

Schadler, S. "Sources of Exchange Rate Variability: Theory and Empirical Evidence." *International Monetary Fund Staff Papers*, July 1977, pp. 253-296.

Solomon, Robert. *The International Monetary System, 1945-1976*. New York: Harper & Row, 1977.

Whitman, Marina v N. "Global Monetarism and the Monetary Approach to the Balance of Payments." *Brookings Papers on Economic Activity*, no. 3, 1975, pp. 491-536.

_____. "Global Monetarism: Theory, Policy and Critique." *Journal of Portfolio Management*, Spring 1977, pp. 7-18.

Foreign-Exchange Markets

Aliber, Robert Z. "Exchange Risks, Yield Curves, and the Pattern of Capital Flows." *Journal of Finance*, May 1968, pp. 361-370.

_____, ed. *The International Market for Foreign Exchange*. New York: Praeger, 1969.

Amihud, Yakov, and Tamir Agmon. "The Forward Rate and the Effective Prediction of the Future Spot Rate," Working paper, Tel Aviv University, September 1978.

Bell, Geoffrey. *The Euro-Dollar Market and the International Financial System*. New York: Halsted Press/John Wiley and Sons, 1973.

Bowers, David A. "A Warning Note on Empirical Research Using Foreign Exchange Rates." *Journal of Financial and Quantitative Analysis*, June 1977, pp. 315-319.

Burt, John, Fred R. Kaen, and G. Geoffrey Booth. "Foreign Exchange Market Efficiency under Flexible Exchange Rates." *Journal of Finance*, September 1977, pp. 1325-1330.

Burtle, James. "Equilibrating the Foreign Exchange Market." *Columbia Journal of World Business*, Spring 1974, pp. 61-67.

Cornell, Bradford. "Spot Rates, Forward Rates, and Exchange Market Efficiency." *Journal of Financial Economics*, August 1977, pp. 55-66.

Dufey, Gunter, and Ian Giddy. *The International Money Market*. Englewood Cliffs, N.J.: Prentice-Hall, Inc., 1978.

Einzig, Paul. *A Textbook on Foreign Exchange*. London: Macmillan, 1966.
_____. *The Dynamic Theory of Forward Exchange*, 2d ed. London: Macmillan, 1967.
_____. *The Euro-Dollar System*, 5th ed. New York: St. Martin's Press, 1973.
_____. *Parallel Money Markets*, 2 vols. London: Macmillan/St. Martin's Press, 1971 and 1972.
Fieleke, Norman S. "Exchange-Rate Flexibility and the Efficiency of the Foreign-Exchange Markets." *Journal of Financial and Quantitative Analysis*, September 1975, pp. 409-428.
Findlay, M. Chapman, III, and E.J. Kleinschmidt. "Error-Learning in the Eurodollar Market." *Journal of Financial and Quantitative Analysis*, September 1975, pp. 429-446.
Folks, William R., Jr., and Stanley R. Stansell. "The Use of Discriminant Analysis in Forecasting Exchange Rate Movement." *Journal of International Business Studies*, Spring 1975, pp. 33-50.
Freedman, Charles. "A Model of the Eurodollar Market." *Journal of Monetary Economics*, April 1977, pp. 139-161.
Frenkel, Jacob A. "A Monetary Approach to the Exchange Rate: Doctrinal Aspects and Empirical Evidence." *Scandinavian Journal of Economics*, May 1976, pp. 200-224.
_____. "The Forward Exchange Rate, Expectations, and the Demand for Money: The German Hyperinflation." *American Economic Review*, September 1977, pp. 653-670.
Frenkel, Jacob A., and Richard M. Levich. "Covered Interest Arbitrage: Unexploited Profits?" *Journal of Political Economy*, March-April 1975, pp. 325-338.
_____. "Transaction Costs and Interest Arbitrage: Tranquil versus Turbulent Periods. *Journal of Political Economy*, December 1977, pp. 1209-1226.
Frenkel, Jacob A., and Gunter Dufey. "The Random Behavior of Flexible Exchange Rates: Implications for Forecasting." *Journal of International Business Studies.* Spring 1975, pp. 1-32.
Giddy, Ian H. "An Integrated Theory of Exchange Rate Equilibrium." *Journal of Financial and Quantitative Analysis,* December 1976, pp. 883-892.
Hendershott, Patrick H. "The Structure of International Interest Rates: The U.S. Treasury Bill Rate and the Eurodollar Deposit Rate." *Journal of Finance*, September 1967, pp. 455-465.
Hewson, John, and Eisuke Sakakibara. *The Euro-Currency Markets and Their Implications*. Lexington, Mass.: D.C. Heath, 1975.
Hinshaw, Randall. "The Euro-Dollar Market: A Comment." *Journal of Money, Credit and Banking*, August 1972, pp. 688-690.
Kohlhagen, Steven W. "The Performance of the Foreign Exchange Markets: 1971-1974." *Journal of International Business Studies*, Fall 1975, pp. 33-39.

Little, Jane Sneddon. *Euro-Dollars: The Money Market Gypsies*. New York: Harper and Row, Inc., 1975.

_____. "The Impact of the Euro-Dollar Market on the Effectiveness of Monetary Policy in the United States and Abroad." *New England Economic Review*, Federal Reserve Bank of Boston, March-April 1975, pp. 3-19.

Logue, Dennis E., and Richard James Sweeney. "White-noise" in Imperfect Markets: The Case of the Franc/Dollar Exchange Rate." *Journal of Finance*, June 1977, pp. 761-768.

Lutz, Friedrich A. "The Euro-Currency System." *Banca Nazionale del Lavoro*, September 1974, pp. 183-200.

Makin, John H., and Dennis E. Logue, eds. *Eurocurrencies and the International Monetary System*. Washington: American Enterprise Institute for Public Policy Research, 1976.

Mayer, Helmut W. "Some Theoretical Problems Relating to the Euro-Dollar Market." *Essays in International Finance*, no. 79. Princeton, N.J.: Princeton University, 1970.

McKinnon, Ronald I. "The Eurocurrency Market." *Essays in International Finance*, no. 125. Princeton, N.J.: Princeton University, 1977.

Mikesell, Raymond F. "The Euro-Dollar Market and the Foreign Demand for Liquid Dollar Assets." *Journal of Money, Credit and Banking*, August 1972, pp. 643-683.

Mikesell, Raymond F., and J. Herbert Furth. *Foreign Dollar Balances and The International Role of the Dollar*. New York: Columbia University Press, 1974.

Riehl, Heinz, and Rita Rodriquez. *Foreign Exchange Markets*. New York: McGraw-Hill Book Company, 1977.

Rogalski, Richard J., and Joseph D. Vinso. "Price Level Variations as Predictors of Flexible Exchange Rates." *Journal of International Business Studies*, Spring/Summer 1977, pp. 71-81.

Schadler, Susan. "Sources of Exchange Rate Variability: Theory and Empirical Evidence." *International Monetary Fund Staff Papers*, July 1977, pp. 253-296.

Syrett, W.W. *A Manual of Foreign Exchange*, 6th ed. London: Sir Isaac Putman and Sons, Ltd., 1960.

Westerfield, Janice Moulton. "An Examination of Foreign Exchange Risk under Fixed and Floating Regimes." *Journal of International Economics*, May 1977, pp. 181-200.

Foreign-Exchange Exposure Management

Abdel-Malek, Talaat. "Managing Exchange Risks under Floating Rates: The Canadian Experience." *Columbia Journal of World Business*, Fall 1976, pp. 41-52.

Ankrom, Robert K. "Top-Level Approach to the Foreign Exchange Problem." *Harvard Business Review*, July-August 1974, pp. 79-90.

Barnett, John S. "Corporate Foreign Exposure Strategy Formulations." *Columbia Journal of World Business*, Winter 1976, pp. 87-97.

Foreign Exchange Exposure Management. New York: Chemical Bank, 1972.

Foreign Exchange Handbook for the Corporate Executive. New York: Brown Brothers Harriman and Co., 1970.

Fredrikson, E. Bruce. "On the Measurement of Foreign Income." *Journal of Accounting Research*, Autumn 1968, pp. 208-221.

Giddy, Ian H. "Exchange Risk: Whose View?" *Financial Management*, Summer 1977, pp. 23-33.

Heckerman, Donald. "The Exchange Risks of Foreign Operations." *Journal of Business*, January 1972, pp. 42-48.

Liberman, Gail. "Two Ways to Measure Foreign Exchange Risk." *Euromoney*, June 1976, pp. 30-36.

Logue, Dennis E., and George S. Oldfield. "Managing Foreign Assets When Foreign Exchange Markets Are Efficient." *Financial Management,* Summer 1977, pp. 16-22.

Olstein, Robert A. "Devaluation and Multinational Reporting." *Financial Analysts Journal*, September-October 1973, pp. 65*ff*.

Prindl, Andreas R. *Foreign Exchange Risk.* New York: John Wiley and Sons, 1976.

Rodriguez, Rita M. "FASB No. 8: What Has It Done for Us?" *Financial Analysts Journal*," March-April 1977, pp. 40-48.

Roll, Richard, and Bruno Solnik. "A Pure Foreign Exchange Asset Pricing Model." *Journal of International Economics*, May 1977, pp. 161-179.

Shapiro, Alan C. "Defining Exchange Risk." *Journal of Business*, January 1977, pp. 37-39.

Index

About the Author

Rita M. Rodriguez is visiting professor at the University of Illinois at Chicago Circle and a consultant with various multinational corporations. She previously taught at New York University and Harvard University. She received the B.S. degree from the University of Puerto Rico and the M.A. and Ph.D. degrees from New York University.

In addition to articles published in academic and management journals, Professor Rodriguez has coauthored a leading textbook titled *International Financial Management* (Prentice-Hall, 2nd ed., 1979), and a reference book, *Foreign Exchange Markets* (McGraw Hill, 1977).